THE LITTLE DARK ONE

THE LITTLE DARK ONE

A TRUE STORY OF SWITCHED AT BIRTH

SHIRLEY MUÑOZ NEWSON

NEW DEGREE PRESS

THE LITTLE DARK ONE
A True Story of Switched at Birth

ISBN   979-8-88926-917-5 *Paperback*
         979-8-88926-960-1 *Ebook*

Disclaimer:
The names of some individuals in this memoir have been
changed to respect their privacy.

To my husband, Scott, our children,
grandchildren, and granddogs

CONTENTS

AUTHOR'S NOTE

God is our refuge and strength, a very present help in trouble.

—PSALM 46:1 (ESV)

Imagine waking up one day to discover everything you've ever known about yourself was wrong. You were living someone else's life and had no idea who you were or where you belonged.

My life was flipped upside down the day before my forty-third birthday, April 7, 2001. I had just received the DNA test results. This test answered questions that I had always had. Up until this point, my life had been a big question mark. Everything, and I mean everything, that I thought I knew about myself wasn't true: my values, the traditions, the way I was raised. None of it belonged to me. I was not whom I thought I was and felt completely numb. The test validated my feelings of not belonging and being abandoned.

It's a devastating and bizarre story, so out of this world that my life even garnered worldwide attention. Everyone wanted to interview me and hear my side of this story. *People Magazine*, the BBC, *Inside Edition*, *48 Hours*, the *National Enquirer*, Dr. Phil, and many more. Many media outlets wanted to share my perspective and my truth.

The world was ready, but I wasn't. All I wanted to do was hide and be invisible.

I was not emotionally capable of talking about it. My whole body was full of shame, resentment, and embarrassment. No way could I publicly speak to anyone, even acquaintances. I declined every interview request. I didn't want to reveal my truth to the world.

My life had been spent feeling unworthy and unlovable. From childhood, I had been taught to suppress my feelings. No one would ever know if I was hurting inside. I was an expert at hiding my pain and anguish. I looked like a well-put-together woman who had her life together.

While statistics show baby switching in the United States is a rarity, it happened to me. I was a wreck. No one could comprehend what I was enduring. I couldn't let anyone other than close friends see me in that state.

For years, I wrestled with the idea of finally speaking to the media, but my fear was still too big. I was afraid of opening myself up to ridicule or criticism.

My son Austin has been pushing me to write this book for the past four years. He told me, "Mom, you need to tell your story. You could help so many people and give courage to others. Look at all you have been through."

I feel blessed that God has given me a voice to tell my story and this opportunity to tell it. I have built up enough courage to share my story thanks to years of therapy and my unshakable faith in God. However, I will be completely transparent in saying I wasn't completely comfortable with writing about my feelings in these chapters at first.

I am a math person who loves spreadsheets. I'm not the creative writer type, but I believe my story tells itself. The details in my memoir are raw and real, and the only reason I am sharing them is to give hope to anyone who has experienced trauma and demonstrate how truly powerful faith can be.

It's easy for me to look back and see all the times God was there for me. Even when I turned my back on him, living a sinful life, God never gave up on me. He laid the foundation for me, carrying me through the lowest points of my life.

In writing this book, I've had to open files with documents, pictures, and newspaper articles, triggering heartbreaking memories from my childhood. I've also had to watch depositions from my court case, forcing me to have vivid flashbacks of painful moments in my life. I am ripping open old wounds that never completely healed. While it has been an emotional journey, I'm grateful for the opportunity it has given me to work on myself, learn about my emotional triggers, and build a closer relationship with God.

The Little Dark One will show readers that with faith, anything is possible. I know my story will help those questioning whether their lives are worth living because I was there, too. This book will give hope to the hopeless. In writing this book, something extraordinary happened to me. I began the process of my healing, and I am getting stronger every day. Nothing is more beautiful than that.

CHAPTER 1

SMILES ON THE OUTSIDE

Be strong and courageous. Do not fear or be in dread of them, for it is the Lord your God who goes with you. He will not leave you or forsake you.

—DEUTERONOMY 31:6 (ESV)

ANTICIPATION—APRIL 7, 2001

The anticipation was killing me. I had been driving home at lunch to check my mailbox for days. I was altering my routine to see if the mailman had stopped by.

I was waiting on one letter that could change my life. A month prior, while visiting my dying father in the hospital, my mother hit me with this bombshell: "Dad wants you to take a DNA test. He doesn't believe he's your father and wants to know before he dies."

As crazy as it sounds, this was an answer to my prayers.

One of my uncles used to call me "the little dark one," not in a derogatory way. More in an obvious way. While I had never considered taking a DNA test, I had questioned my identity for decades. I thought my father would go to his grave, leaving me with the same question I'd had for most of my life: Is James Morgan my father?

I eagerly agreed to take the test.

BIG FAMILIES—1958–1962

In 1958, Gillette, Wyoming, was a small, rural community with a population that was 99 percent white. Large families were typical. The leading industries were farming, ranching, and employment with the Wyodak Coal Mine.

My dad, James, worked as a turbine operator in the power plant at Wyodak and held two part-time jobs to make ends meet. This left little time for him to spend with his family. He was an intimidating man with piercing blue eyes and enormous biceps.

My mom Jean was tall, with dark blonde hair and blue eyes. She stayed home caring for her six kids and was pregnant with her seventh child. When her babies were born, each had blue eyes, fair skin, and no hair.

On April 8, 1958, I came roaring into the world as Shirley Marie Morgan with a head of dark hair, brown eyes, long dark eyelashes, and olive skin. Mom always told everyone I looked just like my paternal French Canadian great-grandmother. I looked nothing like a Morgan baby.

Dad was working and wasn't at the hospital when I was born. To this day, I wonder how shocked he must have been the first time he saw me. I can picture the scene in my mind, Dad walking up to the bassinet to see his newborn baby. Instead, he saw me. He had to be in a state of shock, blinking his eyes a few times. When he opened his eyes, I was still there. Only as an adult did I learn how my birth changed the family dynamics.

My little brother Billy was born on December 8, 1961. He resembled my other six siblings. I was almost three when Billy was born. Hilda was eleven when Billy was born. She was tall for her age and had brown hair cut short. Hilda had been helping Mom with all the new babies. By the time Billy was born, she had become his other mom.

MY FIRST REJECTION—1963

I have very few memories from my early childhood. One memory deeply ingrained in me is so vivid. I can close my eyes and see the look on Mom's face and the tone of her voice. I was around five years old. I had been outside playing on a hot summer day. I ran into the house for a drink of water. Mom was in the kitchen. She had her red lipstick on. That meant she was going somewhere. I wanted to go. I begged, and finally, she relented. It was a rare chance to have time alone with her.

The first thing we did when we got in the car was to roll the windows down. It was sweltering hot, and my legs stuck to the vinyl seats. I was happy and excitedly chattered to the post office.

I got out of the car and shut the door. I heard a buzzing sound and looked up to see a giant bumble bee. I was terrified it would sting me. I ran to Mom, almost in tears, "Mom, look at the huge bee. I'm scared. Will you please hold my hand?"

Her eyebrows pulled together, her nose wrinkled, and her lip curled. With disgust, she said, "No, I won't hold your hand. It's dirty and sweaty."

I was crushed, looking down at my hands. They weren't that dirty. Why wouldn't she hold one? I wanted her to reassure and comfort me, not look at me with loathing. I understand now. This was the beginning of my life of rejection.

SILENCE IS GOLDEN—1964

When I was little, Mom told me I talked too much. I needed to quit telling people everything I knew. Quickly, I learned talking about our personal lives wasn't safe. The older I got, the more cruel and hurtful comments Mom made. She never apologized or explained herself after she said them.

I did what I was taught and shoved all my emotions and questions inside the bottomless, dark pit of despair. I smiled and went on as if nothing had happened.

In 1963, I was five years old. We bought a new house, twice the size of the old one. We had two basements filled with old cast-off furniture, car parts, and broken toys. The basements were filthy. Dad put a coal furnace in the lower basement. Coal was free since he worked at the mine.

At that time, ten people were living in our house. Larry was the oldest son, then Gerey, Hilda, Susan, Tom, Vicky, me, and Billy, in that order. As my brothers grew, they were extremely tall, ranging from six-foot-two to six-foot-six, with large frames, fair skin, blue or green eyes, and blond to brown hair. My sisters were built like my brothers and had the same characteristics. They ranged in height from five-foot-six to five-foot-nine. On the other hand, I am five-foot-four, fine-boned, olive-skinned, with dark brown eyes and hair.

Our house was noisy and chaotic—a constant revolving door and impossible to keep clean. Dad spent the summer working in the yard, making rock walls for flower beds. In the spring, Mom planted flowers, and the yard was beautiful. The outside of our house was always maintained, which contrasted with the inside of our home.

I was like our home, full of smiles on the outside. In contrast, the inside was a plethora of suppressed emotions full of chaos and pain. Whatever my parents told me was a fact—never to be questioned, just accepted, period. Open lines of communication between my parents and me didn't exist. Feelings were things that should be squashed, except for happiness, which we plastered on our robotic little faces in public.

The one adult I felt loved me was Uncle Junior, Dad's brother. He was around six feet tall, with brown hair and kind eyes. He would buy extravagant gifts for my birthday. When it was Vicky's birthday, I, too, would receive a present. Uncle Junior showered me with the love and affection I desperately needed.

When I went to school for the first time, I was terrified. I had never been away from home before. Hilda walked me the block to school. I cried so hard. I didn't want her to leave me. My teacher gave me a monkey with cymbals to play with. Finally, Hilda was able to sneak out the door. I quickly made friends and enjoyed going to school.

I thought our life was normal until I went home with my new classmate. When her dad came home from work, he kissed his wife. They talked to each other, making jokes and laughing. I didn't sense an unwelcome undercurrent like in our house. I was hesitant to have my friends come over to play because they would see how we lived.

A childhood friend once told me, "Your house wasn't the most friendly place in the world. Your sister Vicky was mean to you. I know she was jealous because you were pretty."

Vicky was three years older than me. She was tall, with long, dishwater blonde hair, fair skin, and hazel eyes. Vicky and I were never close; our personalities were opposite.

BLUE-EYED PARENTS—1965

My older siblings would relay their conversation with their biology teacher about genetics at our Sunday dinner. The teacher had told the class, "Two blue-eyed parents could not have a brown-eyed child. It was genetically impossible."

Each sibling would tell him, "Yes, they can. My parents have blue eyes, and my little sister has brown eyes."

Mom, without hesitation, would look at my siblings at the table and say, "Well, he is wrong. Isn't he? Your dad's grandmother was French Canadian. Shirl looks like her."

Why didn't my parents research this information? We had encyclopedias. They could have talked to the teacher. He lived right by us. The comments about me, coupled with this, should have raised red flags. Mom's life was ruled by "Silence Is Golden" and "Ignorance Is Bliss."

BEHIND CLOSED DOORS

My Mom and Dad had two personas—a public one and a private one. Dad wanted our family to resemble the Cleaver family from *Leave It to Beaver.* He was ready to lend a helping hand to everyone. If a neighbor or friend called him for help, he didn't hesitate. Mom would have to wait until he had time to help her.

After leaving high school, I cleaned the top of the refrigerator and found a thank you note from a cousin.

When I read it, I was livid. Dad had helped her with her college tuition. He never helped my brothers pay for college, and his daughters were supposed to get married and have families. For him, work came first, assisting others came second, and his family came last.

Mom's public side was loving and caring. At family gatherings, she helped cook and serve the food. When it came time to clean up after the meal, she helped wash dishes. And she seemed to be happy and social. Later she became everyone's grandmother and babysat some of my friends' kids. At home, she had little patience, especially for Billy and me. We seemed to test her nerves. After eight kids, her fuse was short.

Dad and Mom did not show affection to each other. I don't recall Dad hugging, much less kissing Mom. I don't ever remember getting hugged or kissed by my parents. Our house was devoid of emotional displays of love.

FAMILY GATHERINGS

The times we spent at the family gatherings were the best. Mom and Dad's public side was present. Dad had fourteen siblings in his family, and they were all close. Most of them lived in Wyoming. Each year, the Morgan family had gatherings. My first friends were my cousins, who were close in age to us kids. We alternated celebrating Easter and Thanksgiving between the families. In the summer, we had picnics at Devil's Tower.

Mom was from St. Paul, Minnesota, and had three siblings. They would come to Gillette to visit us. We went to Minnesota a few times only after my older siblings had moved out. They didn't have as many kids as we did. Our car was a four-door. Somehow, we could cram in all eight of us. We were in awe of the big city as they were of the Wild West.

My fondest childhood memories are of the time spent with my aunts, uncles, and cousins.

MY PROTECTOR—1967

We had a Labor Day Morgan family reunion at Story, a small mountain town in northeastern Wyoming, with cousins that we only saw every couple of years. Plus, all of dad's siblings and their kids were there—at least sixty people. Kids were running and playing in the creek.

After playing outside all summer, my skin had tanned to a deep dark olive tone. My hair was black, and my bangs were cut straight across my forehead.

I was on the swing set and looked at the cabin's window. I saw my brother Gerey who was sixteen years old at the time. Gerey was talking to a cousin who was about the same age, and they were looking out the open window. Gerey looked mad. Then I heard my cousin say, "Your little sister looks like a little Indian."

Gerey grabbed him by the collar, yelling, "Don't ever call Shirl a little Indian."

He must have scared the wits out of him. "No, I'm sorry," my cousin said. "I was just kidding."

Gerey looked into his eyes and said, "I don't care what you were doing. You will never talk about my little sister like that again."

I started swinging, smiling from ear to ear. I was proud of Gerey. I felt loved and honored. I idolized Gerey, and at five years old, I was his little shadow. He was tall, with strawberry blond hair, and extremely handsome. All the girls in his class wanted to date him. His hot temper got him into several fights, and his nickname was "Punch."

BOARD OF EDUCATION—1971

In 1970, I was twelve years old and in sixth grade. It was report card time, and I had gotten a D in one of my classes. I thought Dad would ground me, but as I crept up the stairs, I ran smack dab into Mom. She grabbed the report card from my hand and scowled at me, saying, "Just wait until Dad gets home."

Mom left punishment and decision-making to Dad. The waiting was torture. I was hiding upstairs. I heard him stomping down the hall. As loud as he was, I knew I was in big trouble. My heart was pounding in my chest. He opened the bedroom door and shouted, "Get up. We are going downstairs."

Without a word, I followed him to the basement. It was like the death march to me. Without a comment, he bent me over his knees and grabbed his homemade wooden paddle with "Board of Education" carved on it.

I knew if you cried hard right away, it wasn't bad. But I was so mad. I vowed not to cry or make a sound. That made him even madder. The harder he hit, the more determined I was. I scratched down my face so that I wouldn't cry. I thought I would be strong and in control if I didn't cry.

Without a word, he stopped. I could barely stand up. I slowly walked up the stairs. The pain was excruciating. I went to my bedroom and curled up in a ball on my bed. After that, I seldom cried. I thought it was a sign of weakness.

Mom came upstairs and looked at my bottom. She didn't say anything and left. A few minutes later, she was back, "Shirl, pack a few clothes. Hilda is picking you up. You'll stay with her a few days."

I was relieved. As my oldest sister, Hilda was like a second mom and would keep me away from Dad. I said, "I'll be ready in a few minutes."

Hilda would take good care of me. I hurried and packed some clothes. Looking in the mirror, I had bright red welts. Soon they would be black and blue.

When I got settled in at Hilda and her husband's home, Hilda asked, "Shirl, is it all right if I look?"

As she examined the welts, she looked horrified and like she could cry. "I'll get you ice packs," she said.

I had to lie on my side in bed, so I wouldn't hurt. I quickly fell asleep. I knew I was safe at Hilda's house. Unlike our house, hers was always neat and clean.

Before I knew it, Hilda took me home. It was the last place I wanted to go. Dad's beating had taken a toll. I was a different person, and I became withdrawn.

I had refined shoving down my feelings. No one ever knew if I hurt or was sad or in pain. I thought I would be safe if quiet and out of sight. I went that whole month without talking.

I had no one I would trust with my feelings. I did not want to be touched or hugged. It would be a very long time before I let someone hug me. If someone got in my bubble, I would freeze up and panic.

CHAPTER 2

FAMILY DYNAMICS

Drive out a scoffer, and strife will go out, and quarreling and abuse will cease.

—PROVERBS 22:10 (ESV)

FIVE WORDS THAT BROKE ME—1971

I'll never forget the devastation and heartache I experienced when I was thirteen. Mom had a peeved expression, held out a letter, and said, "Shirl, I want you to read this sentence here. Grandma Morgan wrote it to me."

I was puzzled. Why would I need to read Mom's letter? She kept slamming her finger on the one sentence in the letter. After I read it, my heart broke. Grandma Morgan had called me "the nigger in the woodpile." Why did Grandma say that about me? Both of them had told me I looked like Grandma's mom. She was French Canadian. And now this?

True to form, Mom tilted her head, shrugged her shoulders, and turned to walk away. Why would I expect anything different?

As I prepared for bed, I couldn't keep the hurt from coming back up. It was eating me alive, and Grandma's words confirmed I was not worthy of love. I was worthless and didn't want to live.

I put on my pajamas, which were red, my favorite color, beautiful, and full of ruffles. I found a bottle of Bayer aspirin and crawled up to my bed. What reason did I have to live? Did I even belong to this family? Those who should have loved me didn't.

How many aspirins do I need to take to end my miserable existence? I opened the aspirin bottle but forgot to bring a glass of water. I began chewing the aspirins, and they were bitter. I forced one down after the other. I lost count after twenty aspirins and fell asleep. I woke up the following day. My attempt had failed.

I had never fit in with the Morgan family. My appearance and personality were such a contrast to theirs. The undercurrent of not belonging or fitting in had been with me my whole life, and it got worse with each passing year. I was an outsider peering in the window and watching.

I was now aware of the rumors and whispers about my parentage. People in our small town called me the milkman's daughter or the mailman's daughter. Even neighbors speculated Mom must have had an affair. I was the polar opposite of my siblings in looks and personality.

MY WORLD CRASHED—1972

On April 17, 1972, I was in the eighth grade, nine days after my fourteenth birthday. I was called into the principal's office. I was surprised to see my mother's boss waiting for me.

"Get your things and come with me," she said.

"Why?" I asked. "Is something wrong?"

"Just get your things," she replied in a curt tone.

I returned to the office with my coat and books, and we started walking down the stairs. Halfway down, she stopped and then looked at me.

"Gerey's dead," she said. She turned and continued walking down the stairs as if she'd just told me about the weather. I stumbled down the stairs.

I raised my voice, "No, Gerey can't be dead."

I wanted it to be a mistake, but in my heart, I knew it was true. I followed her and got into her car. And I thought, *Why didn't my parents pick me up?*

She told me how Gerey died. He was driving a cement truck for his work, hit a soft shoulder on a dirt road, rolled, and exploded. He was found burned beyond recognition. Knowing this made me sick, and I refused to believe it.

Gerey was engaged, twenty-two, and living life. We would grow up together. But no matter how much I tried to trick myself, this new reality set in.

He was my protector. He always kept me safe from the cruelty I often felt at home and school. And now he was gone.

People came to our house to offer condolences. I had never been comforted, so this was foreign to me. I didn't want to be hugged, yet they tried to hug me as they cried. I was uncomfortable. I needed to be in control of my feelings. Gerey's fiancée must have sensed my distress. She asked, "Shirl, would you like to stay at my home?"

I nodded. It was hard for me to talk without crying. My parents didn't even acknowledge my leaving.

I was lost and abandoned, and I had no self-esteem. Life, as well as my body, was changing. Gone was the tomboy I used to be. Now I was turning into a teen-age girl. My brother was a clerk in a clothing store. He paid me to iron his work clothes. I began ironing all my clothes. People might like me if I looked neat and clean. I wanted to be accepted. No matter what I did, I felt abandoned, unloved, and worthless. I felt ugly, and I hated myself.

YOU AREN'T GOOD ENOUGH—1973

I started high school in 1973. My childhood friend and I would each invite a friend, and we would all hang out on the weekends. He was always kind to me, and his other friend would flirt with me. I enjoyed these nights. On Friday, my mom asked me, "Who are you going out with?"

I told her, and she shook her head. "Don't get any ideas," she said. "His mom would never approve of you. You aren't good enough for him."

The four of us started drinking together on the weekends. I had tasted alcohol before, but now I discovered if I drank enough alcohol, it dulled my pain and inhibitions. I wasn't self-conscious about my looks or not being good enough. I didn't care what people thought of me. As drunk as I got, I could still hear Mom's words, "You aren't good enough for him."

When I was a junior in high school in 1975, I met a guy at the bowling alley. I thought he was such a nice guy, and that turned into a whirlwind of a relationship. Within six months of meeting him, we were engaged. We spent the holidays with each other's families, and I thought things were going well. Until one day in March of 1976, he broke up with me out of the blue.

I was devastated. What was wrong with me? I had graduated in January 1976. I was depressed, and I didn't have anything to do. I was exhausted and would sleep for hours on end. Mom was right. I wasn't even good enough for my fiancé.

CHRIS—1976

In the middle of April 1976, I was throwing up every morning. I knew I was pregnant. I was terrified to tell my parents. I knew they would throw me out of the house. But to my surprise, my parents offered to support me. I finally felt like I belonged in the family.

Ultimately, my dad saw our attorney, and everything was handled. Dad said, "He is responsible for all medical expenses. His name will not appear on the birth certificate. And this baby will be yours."

Chris was born on December 2, 1976. Mom took me to the hospital and sat by my side through my labor. Chris looked like me with dark eyes, long lashes, dark hair, and light olive skin. Mom, Dad, Hilda, and Bill fell in love with Chris. When I found a job, Mom and Hilda took care of Chris.

I worked as a receptionist at the same hospital I was born at. Chris was now a toddler with blond hair, dark green eyes, long lashes, and olive skin. He was adorable and often mistaken for a girl.

I was a failure at relationships. I dated a few guys, but we would break up. One of the guys I had dated had a twin brother named Barry. I met Barry in the bar one night. He was handsome and of average height with a slim build and brown hair. We hit it off, and Chris was an important part of our relationship.

Barry lived in Rawlins, Wyoming, four hours from Gillette, and worked in the oil field. In March 1979, Chris and I were moving to Rawlins with Barry. I talked to my parents about moving. Their concern was for Chris. I assured them I wouldn't work and Chris would be with me.

After telling Hilda, she had a look of anguish on her face and seemed ready to cry. She left without saying a word. The next day Hilda stopped, handed me a thick letter and left.

I opened the letter. It was on yellow legal paper, four pages written on both sides. It was signed, Hilda. She was mad at me for taking Chis away from her. She was more of a mother to him than me. She had taken care of him since birth. Hilda and her husband would give an arm and leg to adopt Chris. Or she wanted guardianship, and I could come and visit him periodically.

I chose not to respond to her letter. From that day forward, our relationship changed. I was now Hilda's adversary. With each passing year, her contempt for me continued to escalate.

A NEW BEGINNING—1979

In the spring of 1979, Chris and I moved to Rawlins. On June 9, 1979, Barry and I were married in Gillette at Barry's family's church. I tried to be the perfect wife and mother. I took care of the finances, shopping, laundry, and cooking. I didn't know marriage was supposed to be fifty-fifty. Little did I know, I was setting myself up for failure.

Barry had a volatile temper. If he got mad at work, he would quit his job on the spot. We had to move for each new job. In sixteen months, we moved three times. The last move was back to Gillette.

Barry forgot my birthday and our anniversary the first year we were married. Every year I would tell myself he would remember. The day would pass, and I would be heartbroken. Without saying anything, I would shove down my sorrow.

LINDSAY—1981

On May 28, 1981, Lindsay was born at 5:35 p.m. Mom was with me through my labor. Lindsay had light hazel brown eyes with long lashes. She had a little bit of blonde hair and fair skin.

I was also so humiliated. Hours later, Barry still hadn't come to the hospital. Finally, I told Mom she should go home. It was getting late. Barry finally arrived and stayed for an hour. He said, "Shirl, I'm going home. You know I have to work."

When he got home, he called me. He was mad and said, "I got a speeding ticket on the way home."

I pleaded with Barry to pick us up from the hospital. He said, "No, I'm working. Your mom can."

Lindsay was baptized in June. The Larsen family and my mom were there. Lindsay was painfully shy, but she always loved going to Grandma Jean's house. Lindsay had brown eyes, long lashes, light blonde hair, and fair skin as a toddler.

T.J.—1984

T.J. was born on January 30, 1984. Barry's employer ensured he was with me to see the birth of our child. Within an hour, I wished he wasn't there. He embarrassed me with crude remarks to the nurses and staff. My contractions were continual, without an epidural. I worried more about what Barry would say next than my severe pain. T.J. had blue eyes, long lashes, a little blond hair, and fair skin.

When I was ready to be discharged, Barry came to pick us up. The nurse told him I wouldn't be released without the insurance papers. He was furious. They were at his office.

In a rage, he stormed out of my room. He returned and slammed the papers on the nurse's desk. With pity in her eyes, the nurse whispered, "You know you don't have to go home with him."

I said, "Yes, I do."

I didn't think I had any other options. I was his wife, and it was my duty. On the way home, we said nothing. Tears slipped down my face. Walking into our home, I was smiling and happy as if nothing had happened.

I had a photo taken of my three children together. No one would ever question if they were siblings. When I received the photo back, I was proud and couldn't stop smiling.

Chris, Lindsay, and T.J. – 1984

To Barry's mom's delight, we attended church every Sunday. I was confirmed in the family church and was an active member.

My kids were my world. I showered them with the love I hadn't received. Our children were clean and dressed nicely, with their hair styled when we went out. We looked like the perfect family if you sat in the pew behind us in church.

All holidays were spent with the Larsen family. We had fun with Barry's sister and husband. I no longer participated in the Morgan family holidays. It was unbearable. When I would walk into the room, all talking would cease. The tension was so thick you could cut it with a knife, and I made everyone uncomfortable.

BIG CHANGES—1988

We bought our first home and started our business in the spring of 1988. Owning his own business was Barry's dream. I was nervous, but he was adamant. Because I knew one day this business would be our children's, we named our company TLC Oil Tools after our kids T.J., Lindsay, and Chris.

I worked at a clinic for surgeons and also did our accounting. I took care of the household duties and our kids. I was busy and needed help keeping up with everything.

Barry made an appointment with an accountant. His name was Scott Newson, and we eventually hired him for our business. Barry's friends had recommended Scott, who was six feet tall, with thinning blond hair and captivating blue eyes. He was athletic and handsome. Toward the end of 1989, Scott called me. He was starting a business and wanted me to work for him. Barry was ecstatic and told me I had to take the job.

Even though I wanted to stay home with the kids and not work, I didn't have a choice. I went to work for Scott. We had a great working relationship. His business grew, and we hired his friend's wife. She was young, and we became close friends. We began spending our time together. She was appalled when I told her about Barry and how he treated me.

"Why do you stay married to him?" She was irate. "He is so demeaning to you."

I replied, "Do you know how often I have been told that? Even from my family."

Barry was jealous of her. He could see the changes in me and didn't like them.

CHANGING TIMES—1992

I seldom argued with Barry. I would do anything to stop a confrontation. When Barry was mad, he would say hurtful things to me. But one night, we got into a massive fight about our kids. I couldn't even talk to him because he was talking over me. I gave up and went to bed.

I made an appointment with our pastor during my lunch hour the following day. At first, we talked about my marriage. The subject quickly changed to my childhood and family. I left his office in tears, feeling I was to blame. I walked into work crying. Scott met me at the door. He hugged me and comforted me. At last, I had someone who listened to me and respected my opinion.

I went in for counseling soon after that. I talked about everything from my childhood to my marriage. I was gaining confidence and a better understanding of how a healthy relationship was supposed to be. Before, I felt lucky Barry even married me. I had low self-esteem and didn't feel worthy of love.

Now, I was finding out I was worth far more. A few sessions later, I realized I didn't love Barry. Over the past year, I had really confided in Scott with all my problems with Barry. Scott showed me compassion I had never felt before. He listened to me and respected my feelings. Scott eventually told me he loved me, and we had an affair.

I filed for divorce from Barry in 1993. I received letters and cards from him, apologizing for what he had done to me, saying he regretted not being supportive or nurturing our love. It was too late. I had spent the last thirteen years suppressing my feelings.

Things didn't go well with Scott, either. In 1994, Scott was separated but still married. I thought we would be together as a couple by then, but he wouldn't commit to a divorce as I had. At that point, we had never been out publicly together, and I felt like a deep, dark secret. I had to quit working with Scott to get away from him. So I left to work for a CPA firm. I ended all communication with Scott in 1995. I was filled to the brim with guilt, but I prayed and asked God for forgiveness.

Time passed quickly, and before I knew it, Chris graduated and went to college. After a semester, he decided college wasn't for him, and he returned to Gillette. Lindsay was a senior in high school, and we didn't see eye to eye on a lot of things. She didn't like my strict rules and expectations, so she chose to live with her dad.

AUSTIN—2000

In the fall of 1999, Lindsay drove out to my office while I was working late, something she never did. I knew something was wrong. She was an emotional wreck when she abruptly said, "You're going to kill me. I'm pregnant."

Lindsay was repeating my life—pregnant and unwed at the age of eighteen. While I wasn't surprised, I was still devastated. But I knew I had to support her just as my parents did for me. I was there for her through it all. I went to prenatal classes with her, and I was at her side when she gave birth to a beautiful baby boy, Austin. I even got to cut his umbilical cord. I was thrilled.

On my way home, I pulled up to a stoplight. When I looked over to the left, I had to take a second look. It was Scott, and I knew it was a sign. I picked up my phone, called him, and told him I had just had a grandson. Scott knew how much I loved babies.

We started talking, and slowly we became friends again. I adored my first grandson and spent every day with him since he and Lindsay lived with me. This was one of the happiest periods of my life.

When Austin was six months old, the stress and responsibilities of being a young mother became too much for Lindsay. Ultimately, I was awarded full custody of Austin.

My life took a drastic turn, but I believed this was God's plan for me.

PANDORA'S BOX—2001

On April 7, 2001, the eve of my forty-third birthday, it was a beautiful spring day, and the flowers were blooming. I was the church treasurer and was at church working on financial statements. I couldn't even concentrate. My mind was focused on the DNA test I had taken. What if the DNA test results were in my mailbox? If they were, would I open them or wait? I finally gave up trying to work. I had to check the mail. Driving quickly to my house, I jumped out of my car and jerked open the mailbox. I peered inside and saw a large manila envelope. I didn't even have to look at the label. I knew it was my test results.

I reached in and pulled the envelope out, turning it over. All I had to do was rip it open. Standing on the sidewalk, I was conflicted. Could I do this alone? As much as I wanted to know the results, I couldn't open the envelope. I was anxious. This document could be Pandora's box. Once open, there would be no way of closing it. I knew I would need the support of my boyfriend, Scott.

My legs felt like rubber as I crawled back into my car. I had to sit there and gather my thoughts. My heart felt like it was going to pound out of my chest. My hands were shaking and sweating as I gripped the envelope. I picked up my phone and called Scott.

"I have the test results," I told him as my voice trembled.

"Shirl, did you open them?" he asked.

"No, I couldn't do it alone. I need you to be with me," I softly replied.

My body was shaking, as was the manila envelope in my hands. When I got to Scott's house, he was outside, pacing back and forth. He rushed to my car door and walked me inside his home. I was a wreck. The moment would change my life forever.

CHAPTER 3

THE TRUTH

The Lord protects the simple; when I was brought low, he saved me.

—PSALMS 116:6 (ESV)

RESULTS—APRIL 7, 2001

I gave the envelope to Scott. My hands and the rest of my body felt numb. I had to know what the DNA test revealed. Looking at Scott with apprehension, I said, "Please open it and put me out of my misery."

It seemed like it took him forever to open the envelope and pull the papers out. Everything was in slow motion except my mind, which was racing with a million "what-ifs." I took a deep breath and said, "I'm ready."

Scott's face looked pensive, and it took him a moment to speak. Without emotion, he said, "James Morgan is not the child's biological father. Probability of paternity: 0.00 percent."

My emotions were all over the place. Mom must have had an affair. What else could it be? Now I knew I was, without a doubt, the bastard child. My life and everything about me were a lie.

Only one person could explain the results to me—Mom. I had to look her in the eyes when I confronted her. I would not let her turn her back on me and walk away like she always did growing up. I had spent a lifetime of her making devastating statements to me and then simply walking away. She never answered or acknowledged important questions. I wasn't going to let her do that to me again. Not this time.

AUTOPILOT—APRIL 7, 2001

I was in absolute shock and on autopilot. What was Mom going to tell me? I had no idea what she would say, and I was running on pure adrenaline.

Before I knew it, I was in Mom's driveway. I walked through the front door with enough force for the door to hit the wall. I could feel the anger boiling in my body. Mom was caught off guard. She was in her recliner reading a book. One look at my face, and she knew I meant business. Perturbed and impatient with me, she said, "What is wrong with you?"

I shoved the paper at her. As she read, her brows furrowed. Her face had a peeved expression as she stood up. She said in a callous, sharp voice, "Well, if he is not your father, I am not your mother. I will take a

DNA test to prove it. I have never been with another man."

At that very moment, I knew there was only one other explanation. As bizarre as it sounded, I must have been switched at birth. Mom would never volunteer to take a DNA test if she had an affair.

We stood a few feet apart as if we were facing off. Mom didn't even reach out to hug me. She just stood there.

It was like she was mad at me. I hadn't done anything. None of this was my fault. I felt as if the air had been sucked out of me.

Her eyes were cold, and she seemed more like a stranger staring at me. She was no longer my mother. From this point on, I would call her Jean. I could not bear to look at her. I grabbed the door handle as pools of tears gathered in my eyes. I pleaded, "Please don't tell Hilda or anyone else about this. I need time to process it."

Jean had that "whatever" look on her face and said, "I won't tell anyone."

I turned away and walked out the door. I knew Jean wouldn't keep this a secret. She told Hilda everything and would be on the phone with her before I backed out of the driveway.

I sobbed uncontrollably in my car and drove to Scott's house.

WHO AM I?

Scott was sitting outside playing with Austin. My eyes were puffy and red from crying. I replayed my conversation with Jean. Scott was speechless as he began hugging me. When he looked down at me, his face was filled with sorrow. He said the only thing he could think of, "I love you, babe. I'm here for you."

I felt so lost. I didn't feel worthy of Scott's love. I told him, "You don't even know who I am. How can you love me? I am an impostor, living someone else's life."

I picked up Austin, and he looked at me with the most innocent eyes. I held him tightly. I needed Austin's unconditional love, and I found comfort in him that I desperately needed.

My children's favorite grandparents were James and Jean, as my children were their favorite grandchildren. I was terrified at the thought of telling Chris and T.J. about the DNA results. What should I say? And how would I say it? When I could finally talk coherently, Scott and I sat down. With conviction in my voice, I said, "I have to find out who I am."

Calmly, Scott said, "We will make a plan tomorrow. Your emotions are raw, now is not the time to make rash decisions."

I knew he was correct, and it was getting late. I went into the bathroom to freshen up. Even though I had just discovered this life-altering news, I looked in the mirror, and my face was the same. The only difference now was I had no idea who I was.

On the way home, I called Chris. He lived in an apartment not far from my house. Trying to sound like nothing was wrong, I said, "Hey, could you please stop by the house?"

He said, "Sure, I'm leaving the grocery store. I'll be over in a few minutes."

I knew T.J. was at home already. I drove up to my house, and Chris's car was there. I pulled into the garage and prayed for God to give me the right words to say. I carried Austin into the house. I could hear the television downstairs. Chris and T.J. were in the living room watching television. I summoned up all the courage I could and went downstairs. They took one look at me and knew right away something had happened.

Chris looked worried and asked, "Mom, what happened? Are you okay?"

T.J. was upset. "Mom, what's wrong?" he asked.

In a calm voice, I said, "I received the DNA test result today. Grandpa is not my biological father."

"What? Are you kidding?" Chris asked.

"No, I'm not," I replied. "I just received the test results. I showed Grandma, and she said to me, 'If he's not your father, I'm not your mother. I will order another DNA test.'

Grandma assured me she had never been with another man, but no matter the results, your grandparents still love you unconditionally. Nothing will change your relationship."

They hugged me, and tears streamed down my face. Chris said, "Mom, it will be okay. I love you."

After Chris left, T.J. was standing with disbelief on his face. The phone rang, and my sister Vicky was on the line.

In a snarky tone, she said, "Hilda and I will have another DNA test done. We'll make the arrangements. It will go to a qualified laboratory this time."

I wanted to scream. Jean didn't care how I felt. Hilda was the last person I wanted to find out. Like everything in her life, Hilda wanted to take charge. How dare they tell me what I'm going to do? This was my life, not theirs.

Vehemently, I replied, "I am *not* having another DNA test done."

Vicky replied, "Well, you still are my sister, and I love you."

I was physically and emotionally drained. I crawled into bed for the night. I prayed, "Dear Lord, I need you and your strength. I can't do this on my own. Please guide me and lead me. Amen."

I closed my eyes, but my mind would not shut off. All I could think about was my life growing up in the Morgan family. I had spent years in counseling dealing with feelings of not belonging and abandonment issues. Now I had validation. I did not belong.

It was impossible to fall asleep with so many childhood memories flashing through my mind. So many things made sense now that I knew I wasn't a Morgan. One memory, in particular, took me back to 1994.

IT'S NOT TRUE—1994

In the fall of 1994, my mother had just returned from visiting her sisters in Minnesota. My kids and I had stopped by her house to catch up. When leaving, Jean gave me the "look" and pointed toward her bedroom. I followed her, and she shut the bedroom door.

In a monotone voice, she said, "While I was gone, did your dad tell you he wasn't your father?"

I looked at her, dumbfounded and shocked. "No."

She turned her back to me and opened the door. Without looking back at me, she said, "Good. It's not true." Jean still treated me the way she had when I was young, dropping a bomb on me without any explanation before turning her back to me and leaving me standing. I couldn't understand where this had come from.

Different scenarios flashed through my mind. What's not true? Why was she asking me this? Was it to hurt me? She could be so cruel to me. Maybe Hilda was mad at me and said something to her. This was Jean's way of shoving a knife into my heart. I wanted to follow her around the house, peppering her with more questions, but I couldn't.

Who am I? Who is my father? I had scenarios running through my head. *Jean must have had an affair,* I thought. Maybe with my father's best friend? What about my father's boss? Or perhaps, my father was my favorite Uncle Junior. That would make so much sense to me. He bought me one of the first eight-track players with Glen Campbell tapes and an expensive cameo bracelet.

When I got home, these thoughts prompted me to write Uncle Junior a letter. I wanted to know if he was my father, and even though I could have picked up the phone and called him, I wanted an answer in writing. I needed the truth in black and white. I even sent the letter by certified mail.

A week later, I was surprised when I received a certified letter from Uncle Junior. He told me in his letter that my question "knocked him off balance." He wrote, "How could you possibly think your mother would have an affair? My answer to you and the world is *no*. Was there any hanky-panky between your mother and me? The answer is *no*."

He told me he would have been proud to have me as his daughter. He explained he had doted on me because I was a blessing from God to him. I had healed his broken heart and given him hope, happiness, and life. I was deeply touched by his letter, and I believed him. But I still didn't know the truth.

I worked hard at staying busy with my kids and work, but I was hurting. On the outside, I looked all put together and in control, but inside I was crumbling. I prayed for answers. I began seeing a therapist every two weeks but still didn't understand why my mother would leave me wondering who my father was.

CONFIRMING THE TRUTH—APRIL 7, 2001

I now realized Jean had to be aware of James's doubts about me for years. That's why she asked me that question in 1994.

I still couldn't believe I had a family out in the world I didn't even know. Thinking about locating my real family was frightening. *What if my biological family rejects me or I can't locate them?* I was excited and apprehensive all at the same time.

I knew my next step. I was ordering a DNA test for Jean. I believed she was loyal to James, and I needed proof.

CHAPTER 4

DESPERATION

Trust in the Lord with all your heart, and do not lean on your understanding.

—PROVERBS 3:5 (ESV)

SUPPORTIVE COWORKERS—APRIL 9, 2001

The next morning, I woke up in the same bed, but I felt totally different. I didn't know who I was, and I had so many questions.

The only thing I knew without a doubt was that James and Jean Morgan were not my parents. Who was I supposed to be, and where should I be living? I had the wrong name. What was my name? Did my biological parents even want me? So many questions, and I needed answers.

I shifted into autopilot as I got my morning cup of coffee. It took all my energy to take a shower. I applied extra makeup to cover my red, puffy eyes. It was Monday, my busiest day at work. I was a controller for a local engineering firm. I also worked part time for my employer's wife, who owned a laboratory testing business and performed my DNA test.

My career began in the medical field and morphed into accounting. It came naturally to me since I was great with numbers. I took college courses and worked in the accounting field. All my hard work paid off. I had a phenomenal job with outstanding benefits, even without having a college degree. God was watching over me. Without my career, I couldn't have bought my house and provided for Austin and my son T.J., who was then seventeen. After Barry remarried, T.J. decided he wanted to live full time with me. I was ecstatic.

I heard T.J. leave for school. I was so scatterbrained I didn't even tell him bye. I managed to drop Austin off at day care. My office was ten minutes from my house. Still, in a daze, I drove slowly to work. I wanted to be late. I couldn't walk into our staff meeting because I was a wreck. One look at me, and they would know something was wrong.

It was quiet when I slinked into the office. Luckily, my office was right by the front door, so I slipped in and quietly closed my door. I sat with my head in my hands and prayed, "God, please give me the strength to make it through this day. Amen."

I was dazed. How could one test forever change my life? If I couldn't comprehend it. How would anyone else make sense of it? I had never read or heard about someone being switched at birth.

Fifteen minutes later, I heard voices in the lobby. I dreaded walking out of my office, but I summoned up all the energy I had left, grabbed the test results, and crept out.

When my coworkers saw me, they were half singing and half yelling, "Happy Birthday, Shirl."

I was so distraught I forgot my birthday was the day before. My sweating hands nervously played with the papers. I couldn't bring myself to look up. I wanted to get this over with quickly. Stammering as fast as I could, "I have the test results. My dad is not my dad. And my mom told me she was not my mom."

The room was silent for a moment. Everyone was astonished. I stood like a statue, afraid I would break down. The room exploded all at once—questions flew from all directions.

"What are you talking about?"

"Shut up. You're making this up."

"How could that happen?"

"You've got to be kidding."

Two of my coworkers were Gillette natives. They knew what my family looked like. So they weren't as shocked as everyone else.

"What the heck? But it makes sense. You didn't belong in that family."

"You stood out like a sore thumb in a family of giants."

Holding back tears, I asked, "Could you please keep this private for a while? I need time and privacy for as long as possible." I knew they would honor my request. We were a family.

Throughout the day, each one popped into my office. They were offering me comfort. I explained Jean's reaction to the test results, and they were appalled. I put my armor on, shoving down the anguish that was bubbling up. God had blessed me with this job and coworkers who surrounded me with compassion.

I made it through the day and was exhausted. I called the lab: "Would you please order a DNA test for Jean."

My employer at the lab responded: "I'm so sorry, Shirl. I heard about it during lunch. I don't understand how it could have happened. Please let us know if we can do anything for you. If you need to talk, please come over."

I was overcome with gratitude. I didn't expect so much support during such a difficult time in my life because I'd never had that before. Before hanging up the phone, I made sure to express my appreciation. "Oh, thank you, all of you have been so kind."

BUM LAMB

I was on a mission to tell James the truth. The short drive to the nursing home didn't take long since I was speeding a bit. As I walked through the doors of the nursing home, the smells of disinfectant, urine, and other body odors immediately assaulted me. As I thought about his response, my heart raced.

The door to his room was open, and I walked right in. As I stepped next to his bed, I gazed over him. He was no longer the strong, intimidating man who raised me. He was now bedridden with rheumatoid arthritis, ravaging his entire body. His legs and feet were swollen with open sores. It was a gruesome sight.

I knew Hilda had already told him the results. A few years ago, she had become the de facto matriarch of the family. Jean could not do anything without Hilda's approval. I gathered all of my strength. In a matter-of-fact voice, I blurted out, "I received the test results. You are not my biological father."

James started rambling on at first. I couldn't grasp what he was saying. He didn't have his dentures in and was licking his lips. With disgust in his voice, he said, "I knew the first time I laid eyes on you that you weren't my baby. Like at the ranch, if we had a black-faced bum lamb, we gave it to a ewe. Even though it wasn't hers, she raised it. Well, that is what I did with you."

I stood there, staring at him. I couldn't believe what he had just said. I was a child, not a lamb. I felt like I had been punched in the stomach.

James grew up on a sheep ranch and was now comparing me to an animal. I had to get out of there. The two people who I thought were my parents had both rejected me.

I had to catch myself as I walked out of his room. My legs were wobbly as I stumbled to my car, and unwanted tears slipped down my face. I began praying, "God, I can't do this. I need your help. Please guide me and lead me. And your will be done. Amen."

I wanted to curl up in a ball and hide, but God told me, "You have children who need you and a home filled with love." I needed to remember that.

BILL

The next day I would tell my younger brother Bill about the test results. He was working at a power plant, just as Dad had. Bill was a foot taller than me, thin with long legs, blue eyes, and blond hair. From childhood, we had always had a special bond. Bill was constantly making jokes and kidding around with me. Bill was always a phone call away, no matter what I needed.

I grabbed the phone and called him. "Hey, Bill, could you stop by my house on your way home?" He agreed to come over.

After the kids and I ate dinner, I paced back and forth, nervously waiting for Bill to arrive. He came walking through the door with a smile on his face. "Shirl, what do you need me to fix?"

I almost laughed, but I shook my head. It was difficult for me to talk, holding back tears. I didn't want to hurt him. "Bill, I have the DNA test results." I paused for a moment. Breathing deeply, I said, "Dad is not my biological father."

He wasn't at all surprised. I thought he would be shocked like everyone else. He laughed and said, "Shirl, I never thought you were my full-blooded sister. I thought Jean had an affair."

I was blown away. This was not the response I expected. Wistfully, I said, "Bill, why haven't you ever told me this?"

"Don't you remember Mom and Dad's forty-fifth wedding anniversary party?" he asked. "When Dad introduced us as 'These are our kids and Jean's.'"

I vaguely remembered the party. We were all called up to the front of the room and lined up in birth order. "Bill, you were standing next to me. I never heard that."

With quivering lips, I asked again, "Bill, why didn't you say something to me?"

He looked ashamed and shrugged his shoulders. I felt like such an idiot. How many other people heard what

Dad had said? I then asked Bill another question. "Do you think Hilda and Vicky heard him say that? Is that why they are so mean to me?"

Bill smiled and said, "No, Shirl. Look at you, and look at them. Does that answer your question?"

IN SHOCK

The next day during lunch, I stopped at my best friend's hair salon. Diane was beautiful with crystal blue eyes and long, dark, big hair, which I was also sporting at the time. We were soul sisters. Our children referred to us as Auntie Di and Aunt Shirl. Why hadn't I called her? I wasn't thinking straight. She should have been the first person I called.

Diane was in the break room. I leaned close to her. Whispering, I asked, "Could we step outside for a minute?"

We went outside and sat down by a tree. The sun felt good on my face as I collapsed on a bench. My nose began tingling, a sure sign of the coming tears. Pleading, I said, "I'm so sorry. I can't believe I didn't tell you of all people. I received the DNA test results, and my life will never be the same." Taking a deep breath, I started to say, "James is not my..."

Diane didn't let me finish. She looked at me as if I had lost my mind. "I already know that," she said. "You stopped here on your way to your mom's house the day you received the results. Don't you remember?"

Diane and Shirley – 2004

Resting my head in my hands, I was shaking and confused. How could that be? I couldn't have stopped. I was
adamant and said, "No, I didn't stop by."

She put her arms on my shoulders and looked into my
eyes, saying, "Yes, you did."

I was bawling as I told her, "I don't remember leaving Scott's house. I was a basket case and had to be on autopilot. I don't even remember driving to Jean's house."

Diane told me in detail, "When you stopped at the salon, I had a client in my chair. You didn't even look like yourself. Your face was pasty white, your eyes were glassy, and you looked catatonic. In almost a robotic movement, you handed the envelope to me and stood still, not even speaking. I wanted to shake you, but you looked so fragile, like a feather would knock you over. I had no idea what was going on. I opened the envelope and read the results. I was shocked, but not really."

Diane continued, "When my clients discovered we were friends, it was like they came out of the woodwork to ask questions about you. And it was always the same question: 'Who are Shirley's parents?' There was no way possible you were a Morgan. Everyone knew you stood out."

Diane told me I eventually left her salon to go to Jean's house. She said I came back fifteen minutes later and told her about Jean's cold-hearted response to the test results. I had no recollection of any of that. It's crazy to think that I could be so distraught and have no memory. I am just so thankful Diane was there for me.

CHAPTER 5

A PLEA FOR HELP

I appeal to you, brothers, to watch out for those who cause divisions and create obstacles contrary to the doctrine that you have been taught; avoid them.

—ROMANS 16:17 (ESV)

After work, Scott and Austin were waiting for me. I couldn't stop talking. I needed to unload this burden. I told Scott about my bizarre conversation with Diane. Scott listened patiently. "Babe, I'm sorry. I don't know what to say."

I hugged him. "You don't have to say anything. I just need you here with me."

"I can't sit here doing nothing," I said. "I need to have a plan. I am on a mission to find my mother."

My mind was racing, and then it hit me. "I'm going to research newspapers at the library."

RESEARCH AND FILES

I printed the library's hospital admissions, dismissals, and birth notices for several weeks before and after my birth-date. It was a little overkill, but I wanted to ensure I didn't miss anything. After Austin was in bed, I turned on the country music channel, made piles of papers, and sorted them. Then I made an extensive spreadsheet compiling all of the information.

I was shocked to find that on April 8, 1958, only Jean's hospital admission and one birth were listed. The story of my birth was a joke in our family. I had heard it from my older siblings countless times. They would laugh and say, "Shirl was born in the hallway."

The story went like this: Jean was in the delivery room. A nurse came in and told her another woman was having complications. The nurse wheeled Jean into the hallway and the other woman into the delivery room. I was delivered in the hallway. Why wasn't the other woman listed?

In the 1950s and '60s, unwed mothers were frowned upon. Their names weren't published in the newspapers with the other birth announcements. That led me to assume my biological mother was unwed because her name wasn't listed in the newspaper.

I was familiar with how to obtain patient records after years of working in medical offices. I went on to the hospital's website, printed a medical release form, and Jean signed it without hesitation so I could open her patient files.

When I walked into the hospital and turned in the form, the medical records clerk said, "We no longer have those records. They are stored in Cheyenne at the Wyoming State Archives."

So Scott and I drove to Cheyenne. A friendly clerk tracked down Jean's patient records and asked what I was searching for. I told her my story. The clerk explained that in 1958, records were filed using a number system. Jean's number was 4734. The clerk said I would need to hire an attorney and petition the state to open patient files 4733 and 4735.

I called Jean on my way home and breathlessly explained what the clerk told me. Jean had even bigger news for me.

Without small talk, she said, "I received the DNA results, and I am not your mother. I will come with you and pay the attorney fees so you can find your biological mother."

Her generosity caught me off guard, but I was thankful because I didn't have the money as a single mother.

But Jean went on to shock me even more. She said, "You can find your mother, but I don't want to know who my daughter is. I want you to give her the Morgan family health history."

I was taken aback. Where did this come from? Why would she not want to find her daughter?

After a few minutes of stunned silence, I said, "Okay, if that is what you want."

I scheduled an appointment with a local attorney to get the petition started. Jean and I met with him, and he explained what we would need to do. Jean and I would be listed on the petition together. I asked, "Is it possible to keep our names private?"

He said, "Yes, in adoption cases, clients' initials are used. I can do the same for your petition."

A BULL IN A CHINA SHOP

In the following weeks, I stayed as busy as possible. My days were filled with taking care of my boys, working two jobs, and volunteering at church. That, coupled with my ability to shove my feelings down, meant I was able to keep my mind off the chaos.

But it felt like the chaos kept following me. In the first week of May 2001, I received a phone call from my son, Chris, who always is in the know about what's happening around town. He said, yelling, "Mom, you won't believe what Hilda is doing. She is going around telling everyone her sister was switched at birth, and she is going to quit her job to find her real sister. Mom, she pisses me off. She will never leave you alone. Besides that, don't you and Grandma have a petition?"

"Yes, we do," I replied. "God only knows what she is up to."

I was irate. I should have known this news was too big to quash. This time, Hilda had pushed me over the edge. She had undermined me my entire adult life.

My paranoia was in overdrive. I already had enough to worry about, and now I had to deal with Hilda and whatever she was up to. I was adamant about keeping my search for my biological mother and anything about who I really was as private as possible.

After I hung up the phone, I just sat there, wondering. I thought about what Diane had told me about her clients questioning my parentage. Then I thought about the comments made whenever I was introduced: "What nationality are you?" "Do you have the same mother? Different father?"

I was startled by my phone buzzing. It was our attorney. "Do you know where Hilda has been?" he asked. "She's been at the hospital, demanding patient information. She has been causing a commotion. I just got off the phone with the hospital's attorney. The hospital's risk management had to get involved, and they are concerned. Hilda was told she could not access any of the patient records. You need to call Jean now. We need to know exactly what is going on."

I was livid. Hilda pushed my buttons. She had no reason to be overstepping. I couldn't believe she even had the gall to go up to the hospital and get involved.

Jean answered the phone. I shouted, "What is Hilda doing? She has been at the hospital raising a commotion, demanding patient files and information. I'm confused. You told me you didn't want to meet your daughter."

Snidely, she replied, "Well, now I do. Hilda is going to find my daughter and her sister. She will do this her way, and we don't need to pay an attorney."

I said, "I'm following proper legal procedures. We have a petition filed, and soon we will know."

Angrily, she replied, "I don't want to do it that way. Hilda has a better way."

I had nothing else to say. Whatever Hilda said, Jean did. There would be no stopping Hilda.

My attorney called a few hours later, "Hilda and Jean just left my office. Hilda told me she would find her sister, and they didn't need my help. Hilda also said her mom was withdrawing from your petition. Hilda had the nerve to ask me when she would get the patient files. I was happy to inform her that by withdrawing from the case, Jean had no legal right to see the patient files, and then they stormed out of my office."

PETITIONING THE COURT—MAY 2001

My attorney called me a few days later. "I spoke with the judge, informing him Jean was withdrawing from your petition. He said when you receive the patient files, you cannot release or divulge any information or the identity or location of your biological mother."

I agreed. I would soon have the files and the protection I needed. I was ecstatic that I could soon have my mother's name. I wouldn't have to worry about Hilda barging into an unsuspecting person's life and revealing this unbelievable news.

Now, we were in the back-and-forth process of legal petitions. I waited for the information daily, but each one would pass by like the day before. Finally, on May 18, 2001, a letter from the Wyoming Archives arrived, saying that the patient files had been sent to the judge.

I was a wreck. The judge now had the information. Why hadn't he released the files to me? All I could do was pray.

About a week later, my attorney called. "The records are to be released on May 24, 2001."

I said a prayer of thanksgiving to God. I was so excited I couldn't stay focused. But when May 24, 2001, arrived, my hope was dashed. I waited all day and never received the files.

While I was desperate to find out who I was, keeping my story and my search for my biological mother private was my main goal.

COUNSELING

I was at my wit's end. It was now July 2001, and I still didn't have the patient files. I made an appointment with my therapist, who had been seeing me on and off for the last ten years. I should have made an appointment with her sooner. By this point, it was difficult for me to function, and I felt bad burdening my friends with my thoughts.

I arrived at my therapist's office and sat in the waiting room. My hands were in fists, and my fingernails were digging into the palms of my hands. My shoulder muscles were so tight you could have bounced a quarter off them. I felt like I had an elephant on my chest. I was overwrought with grief, and I didn't know if I could make it a minute more.

My therapist came out to greet me, and my tears immediately started streaming down my face. I followed her into her office and slumped down on the couch.

Once I started talking, I couldn't stop, "My parents didn't ever love me. James raised me out of a sense of duty. I was switched at birth, and I am an unwanted burden. I can't even get the judge to help me find my mother. Everywhere I turn, I find roadblocks. Hilda is undermining me at every turn. It is like I'm alone, stranded on an island waiting for someone to throw me a life raft. I need help."

She handed me a tissue and lightly touched my shoulder, "Please slow down. I'm here. You are safe. It has been quite a while since I've last seen you. We need to take this one step at a time. Let's start at the beginning."

I was close to wailing. The tears wouldn't stop. I was sucking in deep breaths trying to gain my composure.

In previous sessions, we had lengthy discussions about Hilda and my family. I sighed. "It's still hard to wrap my head around that I was switched at birth. How could it have happened?"

Just one session with my therapist made a difference for me. The more I spoke, the better I felt. My mind was clearing. Even though I'd always placed the blame on myself for failed relationships and things in my life not working out, my therapist put a stop to my negative self-talk. When I told her I felt abandoned by everyone who was supposed to love me—even my birth mother, she interrupted me abruptly.

"Don't do that," my therapist said. "It is not your fault. You were a baby."

I responded, "Do you want to know the strangest thing? I can sing 'Jesus Loves Me' in Spanish, and I can't speak Spanish."

She was astonished. "We don't know what babies hear in the womb, but most importantly, this DNA test has validated your feelings of not belonging and your fear of abandonment. Those feelings are now justified."

Before I left, my therapist said, "Shirley, remember it is not your fault. And if you need anything, call me. It is my job to help you."

"I will, thank you," I said. "I feel much better."

As I left her office, I had a lilt in my walk. I felt free. I didn't know how long it would last, but it sure felt good.

CHAPTER 6

A NAME

*The Lord is my strength and my shield; in him my heart trusts,
and I am helped; my heart exults, and with my song, I give
thanks to him.*

—PSALMS 28:7 (ESV)

RESPONSIBILITY

The months passed by. Austin and I spent most of our
weekends at the golf course with Scott, who was a phenomenal golfer. We went to his tournaments to cheer
him on. It was fun and took my mind off the fact the
judge hadn't released the patient files. I called my attorney weekly and got the same response, "No, I haven't
received the files."

It was Saturday, the first of August. Scott and I were
sitting in the shade on the patio at his house, watching
Austin play. I was on a tirade saying, "You know, my anger
has been centered on the judge. We both know how slow
the judicial system is. I wouldn't be in this position if
the hospital did its job. How could they switch the only

two babies born that day? It should have been caught immediately. They made a terrible mistake and need to be held accountable.

"I spoke with my attorney today. He asked me if I was planning on filing a lawsuit against the hospital. After all this time of waiting for the patient files, I evaded the question. I am beyond disappointed with his ability to represent me. What do you think?"

Scott took a long time to respond. "I wanted you to decide on your own," he said, "I thought about it a few months ago. You have endured so much pain and suffering, all because of the hospital's mistake. I don't think your attorney is the best one to file your lawsuit. There are more qualified attorneys."

I nodded and said, "Then we should research."

When I got home, Chris and T.J. had just returned from a camping trip. I told them about my decision to file a lawsuit against the hospital. Both of them readily agreed. "Mom, you need to. You have suffered all because of a mistake," Chris said.

That night, I fell asleep immediately. I hadn't been able to do that in months. I felt better now that I had made a decision with the support of Scott and my sons and was moving forward.

Scott and I both decided on the same attorney, one of the most famous attorneys in our state. I contacted his office and spoke with one of his associates. Two days later, I received a phone call from their office.

I thought this was good news, but he said, "We can't take your case. The statute of limitations is a problem. But I know an attorney in Casper, Wyoming. If you have a pen ready, I'll give you his information. His name is John Robinson. Whomever you choose, mention our concerns about the statute of limitations."

I was discouraged. Did this mean I didn't have a chance in court? I contacted John Robinson the next day and left a message. He returned my call, and we set up an appointment.

John's assistant greeted us, and she was lovely. I looked around in awe at the artwork and furniture as we waited. When John walked out, he was in his thirties, tall and slim with brown hair, glasses, and casually dressed. I was instantly at ease, and we followed him into the conference room. After introductions, John saw the piles of research I had done. "Why did you have the DNA tests done?" he asked.

I retold my story, and we talked for over an hour, discussing what had transpired. I explained that I wasn't comfortable using the attorney I had retained for records to file this lawsuit against the hospital.

John said, "I would love to take your case. We covered a lot of information today. Please take time to discuss this information. Call me back as soon as you make a decision."

After leaving his office, I felt God must have led me to him. I had decided then and there John would be my attorney, and Scott agreed.

The following day was gorgeous outside. The weather matched my feelings, and I had an air of lightness in my step. I placed the call. "Hi, John, this is Shirley Larsen, and I have decided I want to retain you for my lawsuit against the hospital."

John sounded happy, "Good. We will need to prepare. I'm assuming your other attorney will receive the files. You need to let him know you have retained me."

That same afternoon, I went to my first attorney's office and said, "I'm frustrated with how long this is taking."

Trying to soothe me, he said, "I've been talking with the judge. I think we will have the files soon."

"That's what you told me in May." I was done. "It is almost September, and I still don't have the files. I wanted to let you know I have retained a new attorney for my lawsuit against the hospital."

My attorney was furious, "I have been researching a lawsuit against the hospital. Do you know how much time I have already spent?" He paused, waiting for me to say something. "As soon I receive any information, I will call you. I will send your final invoice as soon as possible."

OUR FAMILY AND OUR DAUGHTER

My sons and I visited James Morgan at the nursing home every Sunday, as was our tradition after church. On this August day in 2001, Jean took me out into the hall right before we were getting ready to leave. With dread, I followed her, and she said, "Hilda has written a letter to the editor of the *News Record*. We want the community to help locate our daughter and sister."

This was the last thing I wanted to happen. I would be humiliated. I felt like I had been punched in the stomach. I begged, "Please don't do that. I don't want everyone to know. I promised you I would find your daughter." Now it would be in the newspaper for everyone to read.

She looked at me with contempt. "You don't understand. This is our family and our daughter. We will do whatever we have to do to find her."

Jean had just summed up what I meant to her. I wasn't her daughter, and my feelings didn't matter. Would there ever be a point in my life when Jean's callous remarks wouldn't wound me?

With veiled bitterness, I replied, "You are correct. This is your family, not mine."

Chris and T.J. were still visiting. I went in, picked Austin up, and left. By the time I got to my car, I was crying. Austin looked at me with innocent eyes, "Nana, sad?" he asked.

I hugged him tightly and kissed his head, saying, "Austin, I'm okay. I love you."

"Love you too, Nana," he tried to say.

We drove to Scott's house, and I was fuming. I turned to Scott and said, "Hilda is going to send a letter to the editorial section of the newspaper about how the Morgan family is looking for their daughter and sister who was switched at birth. How can I stop her?"

He said, "All you can do is contact the paper's editor."

While Austin was playing with Scott, I had time to think. I knew the newspaper editor's name, but I didn't know her personally. I was going to reach out to my best source, my best friend, Diane. I called her, pleading for her help.

Diane said she knew the editor. "I'll call and explain what is happening. I'll call you right back."

Within fifteen minutes, Diane called again. "The editor would like to speak with you. After I told her how the Morgan family had been treating you, I'm pretty sure she isn't going to run it. Let me know what she says."

I was so relieved when I heard the compassion in the editor's voice. She was on my side, and that felt calming.

"After hearing about your story, my heart goes out to you," the editor said. "The letter won't be published."

An overwhelming sense of relief washed over me. I told her, "I promise you if at any time I grant an interview, you will be the first person I speak to. I am so thankful and appreciative."

A NAME

On September 29, 2001, my first attorney called me in the afternoon. He was rude. "I have the name of your mother and grandmother. Do you want me to tell you now? By the way, your new attorney will receive the patient files."

I couldn't receive the news over the phone. I needed Scott's support and preferred to get the information in person. I said, "I will have Scott pick up the information at your office as soon as possible."

Immediately I called Scott. I was so excited I could barely contain myself. I told Scott, "My attorney called. He has the names of my mother and grandmother."

With anticipation, he said, "Tell me, what are their names?"

"I don't know," I answered. "I need you to be with me when I find out. Would you please pick them up for me? I'm just leaving work. I will pick up Austin and meet you at my house."

Without hesitation, he said, "I'll go right now and pick them up."

I grabbed my purse and keys and rushed to the door. I yelled over my shoulder to my coworkers, "They found my mother and grandmother."

I thought I was going to explode with anticipation. I had waited five excruciating months for this very moment. I would hear my mom's name for the first time. I prayed, "Thank you, God. Amen."

I could not think straight. My brain was overloaded, full of the scenarios I had imagined during my sleepless nights.

When Scott entered the door, I almost pounced on him in rapid-fire secession. I asked, "Did you look? What is my mom's name? Please hurry up and tell me. I'm dying to hear."

He slid his pocket knife slowly through the top flap of the envelope and pulled out a single page. I was dying, and he was taking his sweet time. I wanted to rip the paper out of his hands, and then he said it: "Your mom's name is Polly Muñoz. Your grandmother's name is Frances Baez."

CHAPTER 7

DISCOVERY

And my God will supply every need of yours according to his riches in glory in Christ Jesus.

—PHILIPPIANS 4:19 (ESV)

IT'S ALL IN A NAME

I was jumping up and down. God had listened to my prayers. My eyes were glued to the paper. Goosebumps ran up and down my arms, and my heart was pounding out of my chest. I was over the moon. I knew the names of my biological mother and grandmother. I was trying to memorize their names, as they were unfamiliar. The only name that rang a bell was Baez, as in the singer Joan Baez. I have worked for doctors, surgeons, and a CPA firm. Never once did those names cross my desk.

"Shirl," Scott said, "I'm so happy for you. Now you know what your last name should have been."

My brain was in overdrive, and I was pacing back and forth. I began thinking aloud, "Okay, we know this much.

My mother's last name is different from her mother's. This means she must have been married. I could have siblings somewhere."

Scott was listening to me ramble on with all of this new information. "My new attorney, John, will receive the patient files. Polly's admission record would be in the file. Then I will have everything I need to begin my search."

I closed my eyes and silently prayed, "God, thank you for blessing me with my mom's name. And I pray she is alive, and soon through you, I will find her. Amen."

Scott touched my shoulder, "Shirl, remember, we are leaving tomorrow. Have you packed yet?"

My arms came up, and I grunted. "Shoot, I forgot about our trip to Minnesota. I'm way too excited. And yes, Austin and I will be ready to go first thing tomorrow morning."

After I packed for our trip, I lay in bed contemplating how it would feel if I met my mom. Would she want to meet me? Would she be kind and loving? An actual mom to me, like I was to my children. I fell asleep with happy thoughts. I was looking forward to this trip.

Weighing our options, we decided to go to the Mall of America. Scott said, "There is an amusement park for Austin, and you could go shopping. You need to get away from it all for a while."

The shopping part sealed the deal, and Scott liked to shop as much as I did. Scott put bungee cords on Austin's stroller to hold our shopping bags. Scott would do anything in the world for Austin and me. It was hard for me to believe he could love me. Occasionally, my past would haunt me. I felt I was unworthy of love at times. But I knew Scott loved me, or he would have left me when things got rough.

Scott had two daughters whom he adored. His oldest daughter, Jennifer, was two weeks younger than T.J. She was my height and willowy, with long light brown hair and hazel eyes. Leah, his youngest daughter, as crazy as it sounds, looked like me, with long dark hair, brown eyes, and olive skin. Both played on the girls' hockey teams, which Scott coached.

Bright and early the following day, we were on the road headed to Minnesota. My mind returned to my mother's name. I said, "Hey, Scott, if we can't find my mother, should I have another DNA test done? I want to know what nationality I am. Or maybe we could search the internet. I have to know at least that. Now when people ask me, I don't have to shrug my shoulders. I will have an answer."

Scott gave me a funny look and wrinkled his nose. Smiling at me and trying not to laugh. He said, "Shirl, you've got to be kidding?"

Dead serious, I said, "No, I don't know. I've never heard those names before. I can't even pronounce my mother's name. That's why I need the DNA test."

I looked away, slightly hurt that Scott didn't understand. There was so much I wanted to know about my mother. I had a list of questions. Did I look like her? How many children did she have? Where did she live? Or would this be it, her first and last name? Will I even be able to locate her?

"Shirl, Muñoz is a Hispanic name," Scott said, laughing.

I was flabbergasted, "Oh my gosh, how do you know that? The only Hispanic names I knew were from school."

"Remember, Shirl, I went to school in Colorado Springs and was in the minority. If a surname ends with a Z, they will likely be Hispanic. I didn't mean to make fun of you. I assumed last night you knew your mom was Hispanic."

A little aggravated, I said, "Give me a break. There were maybe ten Hispanic kids in my senior class. I didn't take Spanish in school. I didn't know anything about the Hispanic culture."

When we arrived in Minnesota, I put everything I had been thinking about aside and concentrated on having fun. Our hotel was pretty close to the mall, so we spent the whole day there. Austin's stroller was covered with bags. In the car, Scott started complaining, "My feet are killing me. I'm exhausted and need a nap. How about an early dinner? Then you and Austin can go swimming."

Smiling, I said, "You have yourself a deal."

We enjoyed the time together, and Austin had a blast. We loaded up the car and headed home. On the way back, Austin was tired and in a foul mood. Four hours into the trip, he began chucking his toys up front. His binkie was hooked to a little stuffed Pooh Bear, and he hit Scott in the back of his head with it. I shouldn't have laughed. Both of us were pelted with toys. I glanced back at him, and he said, "Nana, we go home."

That was the most extended, most miserable drive home. When we were two hours from home, Austin passed out. Finally, it was quiet in the car. "Scott," I said, "I'm calling John. By now, he should have the files."

I was thrilled as I dialed the phone. When I heard John's voice, without even a hello, I said, "John, have you received the patient files?"

A little hesitant, he said, "Yes. I have good and bad news. Polly's file came, but her admission sheet had quite a few blank spaces. And for the bad news: Hilda's letter ran in the Casper newspaper. I laughed when I saw the picture above the article. Please wait until you see it and read it. I'll fax it to your office tomorrow."

My heart dropped as I said, "I am not surprised. Hilda was on a mission. It's all the better that she could slyly stab me in the back. I don't want my life and story played out in the media. Hilda would love any attention. The funny thing is, she's not the story. I feel like I'm on a roller coaster. I'm high up one minute feeling good, and the next, I'm hitting rock bottom."

At work the next day, I told my coworkers my news. As I walked into my office, the fax was lying on my desk. It was only four pages. I read through each page. What stood out most to me was the box regarding "Financial Arrangements." Polly's form listed "Private Pay," which had been crudely crossed through. And above it was handwritten "Welfare." A box to the right had a checkmark for Welfare.

John was correct. The form had her name and date of birth. Ironically, Polly's birthday was eight days before Jean's, so it was a day I would remember. She was twenty years old. She listed her mother as an emergency contact. The other pages were hospital notes written in medical jargon. I could only decipher that she had blood transfusions and was given Demerol.

But this was a start. I would go back to the library. They had all of the Campbell County high school yearbooks. She might have attended school in Gillette. I said a prayer: "Dear Lord, please let me find her picture in the school yearbooks. I'm desperate. This might be my only chance. Amen."

SHIRLEY, THE PRIVATE INVESTIGATOR

Now, for the dreaded editorial. John was correct. The picture above the editorial was a sketch of two women looking at each other with a shopping bag in between them. They looked like cartoon characters, and I got a chuckle.

The heading was: "Are You My Sister?" In part, it read: "Jean Morgan gave birth to a daughter in Gillette on April 8, 1958. DNA testing revealed that they did not go home with their biological daughter. And she could have been adopted at birth." It ended with: "We are reaching out. Going public has been a hard decision as we are pretty private people."

After I read the last comment, I felt like throwing up. I was devastated that now everyone would know I had been switched at birth. The whole thing was hokey. Private, my foot. Hilda had blabbed this story to anyone who would listen. Nothing was private about the search she was pursuing.

When lunchtime rolled around, I went to the library. I knew exactly where the yearbooks were. I sat on the floor, took the 1956 to 1958 yearbooks off the shelves, and put them on a table. Polly wasn't in the 1956 yearbook. I picked up the 1957 yearbook. I found Polly's name, and when I saw her picture, it was a good thing I was sitting in a chair, or I would have fallen. My heart was racing as I fixated on her features. It was like looking in a mirror. We had the same-shaped eyes, eyebrows, the same smile, and dark hair. I didn't need a DNA test to prove it. This was my mother.

My face must have lit up with pride, smiling from ear to ear. I wanted to jump and show everyone in the library, saying, "This is my mom." I couldn't take my eyes off Polly. I wished Scott and Diane had been here with me.

I began paging through the yearbook. Her photos were in the Pep Club and Allied Youth Members. It was like a dream, and someone needed to pinch me. I wondered why she was a freshman at nineteen years old. Later, I would find out that Polly's family were migrant workers, and she had missed two years of school.

Then, I looked at the 1958 yearbook. I found her sophomore class photo. Her dark hair was styled in a bob cut, and she wore a choker necklace. I could picture her in a poodle skirt with black-and-white saddle shoes. I paged through the rest of the yearbook. She was not active in school clubs. I assumed it was because she was pregnant with me.

Polly's address wasn't listed on her admission form. She went to high school in Gillette. I wanted to see where she had lived because I knew it would make me feel like a part of her. I was floating on cloud nine as I called Diane. Breathlessly, I said, "Guess what? I found a picture of my mom, and I look just like her. Can you believe it? Now, I need to find out where she lived."

Remember, this was 2001, and my research was done in an old-school fashion. We had a Gillette museum, which might have old telephone books. I ran outside to my car and was on my way to the Rockpile Museum. I asked the clerk at the museum if they had telephone books from the 1950s. The clerk looked at me astonished and said, "A woman was just in here. She asked the same question."

CHAPTER 8

POLLY

Therefore I tell you, whatever you ask in prayer, believe that
you have received it, and it will be yours.

—MARK 11:24 (ESV)

AN ADDRESS

I knew the clerk was referring to Hilda, but I had to forget
about her. I had way more important research to do. I found
both Polly and her mother and their addresses in the vintage
telephone books. I wrote the addresses down on paper and
drove up and down the streets on the east side of Gillette,
looking for the houses. I couldn't find them. I assumed they
must have been torn down. I felt defeated again.

I called John to let him know I had found Polly's yearbook
photos and her addresses. He asked, "Shirl, could you go
back to the library? Recheck the yearbooks and see if
you know any of her classmates who still live in Gillette."

So back to the library, I went. I was a Gillette native
and familiar with old family names. I found quite a few

classmates still living in Gillette. I jotted down their names and called John back. He said, "I'm going to contact a private investigator and give him this information."

Within a few days, John called me again. He sounded optimistic, "In 1960, Polly lived in Worland, Wyoming. Our investigator feels certain he will locate her. How would you like to handle it? You could have a third party talk to her first, and Polly could decide if she wants to meet with you."

I could not take another face-to-face rejection. In a solemn voice, I said, "I want a third party to tell her. I don't want to burst into her life without any warning. Saying, 'Hi, I'm your daughter. You took the wrong baby home.' I couldn't hit her with the devastating, life-altering news. I have known for five months, and I'm still trying to wrap my head around it."

Wow, I couldn't get over how fast this was happening. After waiting so long, I had almost given up. Overwhelmed, I had a hard time grasping this incredible story. Polly had lived two and a half hours from me in 1960. I was overjoyed. What were the chances Polly still lived in Worland?

RESULTS FROM ONE LETTER

After work, I received a phone call from one of the Morgan sisters. She said in an enthusiastic voice, "We found our sister. An adoption intermediary read Hilda's editorial in the Casper newspaper. And within a few hours, she found our sister."

After a moment, I mumbled, "Okay." I was stunned and hurt, not able to speak.

Hanging up the phone, I wanted to know how it was possible. That one letter would lead the Morgans to their daughter. I followed proper legal channels, abiding by the court's rules. Yet the Morgans had information the judge ordered confidential. And Hilda had my mother's name before I did. I felt like smoke was pouring out of my ears. I was angrier than ever.

Great, now my worst fear had come true because Hilda had the information. I felt physically violated and terrified of what Hilda would do. I needed to vent before I blew up. I called Scott, yelling as I replayed the conversation. He wanted to know how this transpired. I shouted, "I don't know, some intermediary found the files. And came in to save the day."

Scott tried his best to calm me down, "You know there is an upside to this. Suppose the Morgans had the information about their daughter. That means you will also have the information and be able to locate your mother."

"Thank you," I said, "I needed to hear that. I was fuming mad. Thank you for keeping me centered. That is one of the things I love about you."

The following day, John called, cheerful, "I've just spoken to the woman you were switched with. Her name is Debra. Your mom, Polly, lives in Tremonton,

Utah. I asked Debra if you could call her. She gave me her number and said you could call if you wanted to."

I sat at my desk with my head in my hands and was in a quandary. I looked at Debra's phone number. Did I call her now or wait? The sooner, the better. Maybe she hadn't spoken with Hilda, and I would have a chance. Call it paranoia, but I knew if she talked to Hilda, Debra wouldn't speak to me.

Then joy overtook me. I was upbeat, with thoughts circling in my head. Oh my gosh, I will talk to the person I was switched with. Debra could have the same feelings and issues I have had. We could become best friends, spending time together and talking. I envisioned many late-night talks filling in each other's blanks. Who else in the world would feel as I do? Only Debra would. I was eager to call her now that I had such high hopes. Yet this tiny voice in my head told me to be prepared. Debra might not want to speak with me.

I picked up the phone and started to call, only to put the phone back down. This went back and forth with what-ifs. I had to stop and make the call.

DEBRA
I dialed the number, and the phone rang. My heart was in my throat as I waited. When Debra answered the phone, we introduced ourselves to each other. I was bubbling over with excitement.

"I am excited to speak with you. I still can't believe I am talking to the person I was switched with. The only person who could relate to me. I know we will have a lot in common."

With skepticism in her voice, Debra replied, "Yeah, I did talk to John, and he said you might be calling. I can't believe it is really true. Polly has always been my mom. I don't understand how this could happen."

Her voice was almost childlike. I had assumed the intermediary had explained everything to her. But it didn't sound like it, and I was dying to ask a million questions. Slowly and patiently, I went through how this had transpired. I continued, "You have six siblings. Larry is your oldest brother, fifty-four years old. Next is Hilda, Susan, Tom, Vicky, and Bill, the youngest, who is forty. You fall in between Vicky and Bill."

Debra replied, "A woman called me and told me I had been switched at birth. I don't understand any of this." She would repeat this phase throughout our conversation. "I called my mom, and she didn't believe it when I told her. She told me they were wrong. She was my mother."

I almost lost it. I tried to soothe her, "I know this has to shock both of you. DNA tests are an undeniable fact. I have waited five months to find out who my biological mother is."

Debra reluctantly said, "*My* mom's last name is Leyva, and she lives in Tremonton, Utah. She is married to Juan, my stepfather. I have a sister Benita who lives in Worland. My brother Craig lives in California. My mom and I are very close. She has always cared for me. She tried to protect me from my stepfather Juan. He is a mean man with a bad temper."

Debra's voice seemed to change constantly. She spoke passionately regarding Polly and sounded as if she were filled with rage as she mentioned Juan. She made it clear Polly was her mom. It was like a child calling dibs on something.

I wanted to meet my mom Polly as soon as possible. Unable to contain myself, I burst out, "I want to meet my mom as soon as possible."

"Oh," she said, "*so* you haven't talked to her yet?"

I felt like she was rubbing salt in a wound. Calmly as I bit my tongue, I answered, "No, I haven't. John didn't have Polly's contact information."

Debra seemed happy I hadn't spoken with Polly. She said, "Well, I'm coming to Gillette. To meet my *mommy and daddy*. First, I'm going to visit my mom in Utah. Then I'll go to Gillette. I can't wait to see *Mommy and Daddy*."

Now she sounded happy and wanted to meet her parents. I thought *"Mommy and Daddy"* was what a child would call her parents, not a forty-three-year-old woman. After she told me this, I panicked. Debra meeting Hilda first would be a disaster. I could only imagine what she would say about me. What if Debra, in turn, told Polly? I was desperate. I had to meet Debra first before she had a preconceived notion about me. What if Polly refused to meet me?

I was going to be cheerful. "It would be fabulous to meet you and my mom in Utah," I told her.

Hesitating for a long moment, her voice changed again. I detected a deceptive tone, "Yeah," she said, "I don't have any idea when I'm leaving."

I tried to change the subject quickly but had gone too far. I said, "I have pictures of your family. Would you like me to email them?"

Debra said, "Yeah, sure."

Her response shocked me. Suppose I was given a chance to see family photos. I would be jumping up and down with unconstrained delight.

Paranoia gripped me. I said, "Debra, I would appreciate it if you don't mention our phone conversation to the Morgan family."

Replying in a flat tone, "Oh, okay." And she gave me her email address.

Trying to sound happy, I said, "It was wonderful speaking with you. I look forward to meeting you and getting to know you. I'll email the photos to you."

Our phone conversation ended abruptly. I thought I blew it, sounding crazy and suspicious. She probably would never speak to me again. I gathered the pictures and emailed them to Debra. The email bounced back. I must have had the wrong address. I called Debra back, but she didn't answer her phone. I left her a message, and she never returned my call. My gut feeling was correct. I have never had another conversation with her. The relationship I craved would never come to fruition.

I was kicking myself. I felt horrible. Had I ruined our chance to become friends? Debra was my only chance to speak with someone I could relate to.

A MOTHER'S CALL

The next night my phone rang, and a low voice said, "Hello, is this Shirley?"

I replied, "Yes, this is she."

What the woman on the phone said next blew me away, "This is your mother, Polly."

I was in a state of shock. I had waited for this moment, and now I was speechless. I hadn't prepared myself for this phone call. I couldn't mess this one up. This was the first time I would be speaking with my mom, and I needed to make a good impression.

I exclaimed, "Oh my gosh, I cannot believe I am finally talking to you. I thought I would never find you, and now I am speaking with you."

Scott had a look of surprise on his face and mouthed to me, "Your mom?" I nodded.

Polly sounded horrified. "I am in shock," she said. "Never once did I think that Debbie was not my child. Her biological father was white, and I thought Debbie looked like him. I don't understand how this could have happened."

That wasn't the reaction I wanted to hear. I felt like the little girl on the sidewalk again, but now my biological mother was rejecting me. I wanted her to tell me she was happy to find out I was her daughter. Instead, she sounded angry. I wanted to cry.

I didn't know how much Polly knew, so again, I replayed the story that led us to this moment.

Polly was in denial, saying, "How can this be?"

What could I possibly say to her? This wasn't my fault. I felt like everyone was blaming me. I wanted to scream, "I was a baby. This was not my fault."

Sympathizing and trying to understand what a shock this was to Polly, I spoke compassionately and told her about the story I had been told about my birth and the woman who had a difficult delivery.

Polly replied, barely audible, "That must have been me."

She still sounded upset. I continued, "I went to the library and began researching old newspapers. Only one baby was listed that day, and it was me. Given that it was 1958, I assumed an unwed mother would have given her baby up for adoption."

With love, she said, "She was my baby. I loved her. I would have never given her up for adoption."

Polly spoke lovingly about her baby. She didn't say I was her baby. She meant Debbie was her baby. That statement warmed my soul and hurt me all at the same time.

The sense of not belonging had plagued me my entire life. I wanted to belong. I was determined. I had to meet her to fill the void in my life. I tried to sound pleasant, "I would love to meet you as soon as possible."

Polly was quiet. My heart was pounding in anticipation as I strained to listen. "My husband Juan is mad about this whole thing. And if you came here, he would be even madder."

I was frantic. I wanted to meet her. To feel her arms embracing me. Now pleading, "I will fly there and stay in a hotel. You could come and visit me. He doesn't even have to know I'm there."

I felt like my life was repeating itself. I was not accepted or acknowledged by anyone.

Polly said in a worried tone, "No, you can't. Juan would find out, and he would be mad at me. I must let him cool down first and call you later."

Our call ended. I was trembling and crying as I said to Scott, "Polly won't let me visit her, and she sounded mad at me. I was happy when she first called and said she was my mother, but it went downhill from there. She was afraid her husband would hear her talking to me. I felt she was ashamed of me. I have to meet her, what am I going to do? She was adamant I couldn't come."

Scott softly said, "Shirl, it sounds like she is scared of her husband. He could be abusive. She could be concerned for your safety."

Polly did sound scared. Maybe Scott was correct. After he left, I picked up Austin and his favorite blanket. I held him close, smelling the scent of baby lotion. He fell asleep as my tears fell upon his head. I prayed, "God, thank you for the precious gift of Austin, and now I have found my mom. I pray you will be done. Amen."

I felt abandoned again. My biological mother didn't want to meet me. I understood this was traumatic for Polly. Yet I believe I would have embraced another daughter if I were in her place. Would we ever have the mother/daughter bond? Did she even want to meet me? This was the story of my life, rejection after rejection.

CHAPTER 9

SIBLINGS

I have chosen you and not cast you off; fear not, for I am with you; be not dismayed, for I am your God; I will strengthen you, I will help you, I will uphold you with my righteous right hand.

—ISAIAH 41:10 (ESV)

MEETING MY FAMILY

Navigating the judicial system takes time. The first week in October 2001, I was making progress. John, my attorney, called. "Shirl, I have your aunt and siblings' phone numbers. And how are you doing?"

Sadly, I said, "Polly wasn't very receptive to me. I think she is terrified of her husband. But I pray my aunt and siblings will want to meet me. I can't wait. I'll reach out to them today."

Before I made the call, I prayed, "God, please help me. I don't know what to say when I make these calls. Please give me the words I need. Amen."

Craig lived in California. Even though I was nervous, I decided to call him first. "Hello, this is Shirley Larsen. I'm not sure if you have any knowledge about me. Debra and I were switched at birth, and I just found out I have siblings. You are my half brother."

Craig said, "Yes, I spoke with Debbie, and she is devastated. My family is planning a quick trip to Worland. We will be there on the weekend of October twelfth. We could meet then."

Eagerly, I replied, "I would love to. Let me check with my boyfriend. I'm looking forward to meeting you and your family. And I'll let you know once we firm up our plans. Thank you."

The call was short, but I was pumped. The timing was perfect. God's hands were at work.

I made a quick call to Scott. Without hesitation, he said, "Sure, we can leave early Saturday morning."

I felt fortunate to have Scott pushing down my insecurity. Feeling more confident, I called my half sister. Benita answered her phone, and she sounded happy. I repeated what I had said in the call to Craig. After the mess I had made with Debbie's call, I needed these relationships to succeed. Upbeat, I said, "I just spoke with Craig, and his family will be in Worland the weekend of the twelfth. Scott, my boyfriend, and Austin, my grandson, and I will be there Saturday morning. And I would love to meet you."

Benita sounded a little doubtful. "This has been crazy. I never questioned that Debbie was my sister. And no matter what, she will always be my sister."

I thought about how lucky Debbie was to have a family that still supported her. I felt a pang of jealousy. I said, "This has been a difficult time for all of us. But now it is exhilarating. I can't believe I'm going to meet my biological family. Saturday won't come soon enough."

Feeling like I had won the lottery, I called Aunt Mary. After the introductions, she sounded kind and loving. I repeated what I had said in the calls to Craig and Benita. My prayers were coming true. I felt like I was walking on water.

Aunt Mary, gentle and reassuring, said, "It is hard to believe this happened. I always thought Debbie looked like her dad. And now this. First, I got a call from a lady. I didn't catch her name, and she asked me if I knew Debra DeLay. I said yes, she is my niece. At the time, I knew Debbie was looking for a job. I assumed this call was about a job. I told her she lived in Arizona and didn't have her phone number. And the rest is history."

I replied, "Craig and his family will be in Worland. Will you be around on Saturday?"

She said, "I'll be at work. I want to see you in person. We own a pharmacy, and it's in Blair's grocery store. You will drive by the store when you get into town. I would love it if you stopped in."

With so much excitement, I said, "That will be our first stop. I'm looking forward to meeting you on Saturday."

I had a positive feeling about Aunt Mary.

MY FAMILY

Finally, Saturday arrived, and we were on the road bright and early. I talked endlessly about meeting "my family." Scott, however, was apprehensive, "I hope they are your family. I don't want you to be hurt again."

I replied, "I am happy, and I know this is my family. You wait and see."

Ten minutes outside Worland, I called Aunt Mary, "Hi, this is Shirley. We'll be there in a few minutes. I can't wait to meet you."

As the doors glided open, I could smell fried chicken. The grocery store must have had a deli. I stood for a moment, looking around to find the pharmacy, which was in the very back of the store. That is when I saw a petite Mexican woman smiling as she approached me. The first words out of her mouth were, "You look just like your mom."

I had tears in my eyes, momentarily speechless. This was new to me, a true sense of belonging. What a marvelous feeling it was. Smiling, I said, "You have no idea how much that means to me. I have never in my life been told I resembled a family member. Quite the opposite was said about me."

Aunt Mary smiled. "It is great to meet you. I have no doubt you are Polly's daughter. I need to get back to work, and I'll call Benita to let her know you will be waiting in front of the store. I'll stop by after I get off work."

Enthusiastically, I said, "Thanks. It was so wonderful to meet you. I look forward to visiting with you later."

Scott and I turned to leave. I looked over my shoulder, and Aunt Mary was quickly walking away. I thought, wow, she walks as fast as I do.

Through tears of happiness. "This is my family," I said. "I can't believe this is *my* family."

Benita was there in ten minutes. She exited her car, and the first thing I noticed was her thick, long, beautiful black hair. She was shorter than me and pretty. We followed her, and when we walked into her home, it smelled so clean and fresh. Her walls were decorated similarly to my home. Benita introduced us to her fiancé and three daughters.

We all went outside to enjoy the warm fall day. I was standing next to Benita. I said, "I love fall. It's my favorite season, and the changing of colors is amazing."

I told her that her daughters were pretty and looked happy. Benita replied, "Thank you, I stay at home with them. Would you like to go back inside where we can have a quiet conversation?"

"I would love that," I said, wanting to know more about my family and trying to take in everything around me. I asked, "Did you notice we both are wearing red shirts? My home has the same color theme as yours. Isn't that ironic?"

Benita looked down. "I didn't even notice," she said. "I'm still blown away. How in the world did this happen? It's crazy. How could the hospital mix up a Mexican baby with a white one? It just doesn't make any sense."

I had told the story many times. I explained it in detail to Benita, "I know only two babies were born that morning," I said, "yet they couldn't keep us straight. I can't comprehend how it could happen either."

The topic changed to our children. "I also have three children, Chris, Lindsay, and T.J., four including Austin. I was the youngest daughter, and now I'm the oldest daughter. My life has been flipped upside down, and I'm sure Debbie feels the same way."

Benita frowned, "Debbie is having difficulty dealing with everything. But it won't change our family's relationship with her. Mom loves her, and Debbie will always be her daughter."

Okay, this wasn't going well. I felt like an intruder, and Benita was marking the territory. I changed the subject: "Is Craig planning on coming over?"

Benita's mouth turned down, "No, we aren't close."

How could I change the subject again? I felt beads of sweat on my face. I couldn't seem to find a safe topic. I glanced at her coffee table, where a stack of photo albums sat. Benita noticed. "Would you like to see pictures of our family?" she asked.

Benita handed me an album, and turning the pages was like a dream. It was surreal looking at pictures of my biological family. And I had no idea who they were, and a rush of sadness swept over me. I had found my family, but I had so much to learn. I had lost forty-three years of Mexican heritage and traditions. I didn't think making up for those lost years would be possible.

I turned the page and was speechless—a photo of a girl in her late teens. She was tall with long hair, it looked blonde, but it wasn't a color photo. I was staring at a girl who looked exactly like Vicky. Benita must have registered the shock on my face, "That's Debbie," she said.

I exclaimed, "Debbie looks like a twin of her sister Vicky."

It was so uncanny. Debbie and I both resembled our biological families.

Next, I saw a photo of Benita with a little boy. I thought Craig and Benita were closer in age and asked, "Benita, is that your brother Craig?"

Shaking her head, "No, that is my little brother Jon. He is twenty-one years old now. You didn't know Mom has four kids?"

I was curious why Debbie had not mentioned Jon when we spoke. With raised brows, I answered, "No, Debbie only mentioned you and Craig. My son Chris is four years older than Jon. To think Polly had Jon a year before I had Lindsay is crazy." Looking at my watch, I said, "I probably should call Craig and firm up our plans."

Benita looked uncomfortable and said, "We should go outside with everyone else."

Outside, Scott, Austin, Benita's daughters, and fiancé were sitting in chairs visiting. I walked over to the other side of the yard for privacy, knowing how Benita felt about Craig. I placed the call, and Craig picked up immediately. I began, "This is Shirley. What time would you like us to stop by?"

He said, "I'm doing research and should be done in an hour or so."

After we ended our call, a man stepped out of his truck and walked right up to me. He was a short Mexican man with graying hair and a kind face. Before introductions were made, he hugged me. With a twinkle in his eyes, he said, "Hi, I'm your Uncle Felix, Aunt Mary's husband. Welcome to the family."

Tears filled my eyes, "Hi, Uncle Felix. It has been an amazing day for me. Meeting my real family, I'm in awe. I thought this day would never come."

We visited for a while before Aunt Mary stopped by. "Shirley," she said, "I can't believe how tall you are. It is wonderful to meet you. I wish Polly were here."

Aunt Mary and I discussed the story. It still felt surreal, no matter how many times I told it. Aunt Mary smiled, saying, "Next time, you must stay longer. I want you to meet my two daughters. I have two sons. Both moved after college. Kim, my youngest daughter, looks just like you. She has a store downtown called "Petals and Pages." I know you two would hit it off."

I felt an instant connection, and I loved my Aunt Mary. I said, "I can't wait to meet Kim. I plan on coming back real soon."

My phone beeped, and Craig was ready. Disappointment washed over me. I wanted to stay and keep visiting with Aunt Mary. "Craig texted me," I said. "We are going to meet his family at their hotel. You have my phone number. Call me anytime."

At the hotel, Craig and his family were seated around a table. Craig stood up to shake our hands. He held himself stiffly as if this were a business meeting—a stark contrast to our last visit.

He introduced us to his family. Craig explained, "I'm in Worland researching my genealogy."

We made uncomfortable small talk, took a few pictures, and said goodbye. It was awkward, and I was glad it was over. That would be the only time I would see or speak to him.

On the way home, Scott and I talked. "That was a stilted meeting," I said. "It was the opposite of our visit with everyone else. Now, do you have any doubts if this is my family?"

Scott said, "Okay, you got me there. Yes, it is your family. Craig didn't appear to be overjoyed meeting you. But, hey, the positive thing is you went from being the shortest to one of the tallest in your biological family."

Laughing hard, I almost cried. "I went from being the youngest and shortest daughter. Now I'm the oldest and tallest daughter. Isn't that crazy?"

A MOTHER'S REQUEST

A few weeks later, Jean called. "I want to invite you, Scott, and the kids to a party," she said. "Family and friends will gather at the nursing home to celebrate Debra."

Sighing, I said, "I'm busy at work, and we probably won't come."

The phone call ended, and I was hurt, angry, shaking, and wanted to cry. How could she do this to me? It was like rubbing salt in a sore. I meant nothing to her. Horses couldn't drag me to that party. I was humiliated, and I didn't want to show my face. How could a mother who raised me for forty-three years invite me to her real daughter's party?

I was no longer a Morgan. I had to let go and let God. It was tearing me up. I prayed, "God, please help me and give me strength. Amen."

Taking a deep breath, I called Scott and told him about Jean's invitation. He was on fire. "Don't you dare go to that party," he said.

Luckily, I was really busy at work, and my mind was occupied.

Later that week, Polly called. I was excited and told her about my trip to Worland and whom I had met. Polly sounded serious. "You be careful of Benita," she said. "She tends to cause many problems. Watch what you say to her."

It felt good she was concerned about me. "Thank you. I will be watchful of Benita."

Polly said, "I almost forgot the reason I called. Debbie will be in Gillette. The Morgan family is having a big party in her honor."

Exasperated, I said, "Yes, I heard about it. We aren't planning on going."

Polly was shocked at my answer. And said sternly, "You really must go to the party."

I said a quick prayer for patience. I had to make a good impression. This was my mom, Polly, telling me to go. How could I say no? Grudgingly, I said, "Okay, we will go."

The moment those words were out of my mouth, I knew this would be a huge mistake. But I desperately needed Polly's approval. I felt stuck. Scott had heard my part of the conversation. He was shaking his head furiously.

"I cannot believe you told Polly you would attend that party. Shirl, why do you want to torture yourself? You know what will happen. Why are you allowing yourself to be hurt again and again?"

Tears slid down my cheeks. I sadly said, "I have no choice. Polly asked me to go. How could I refuse her? I need her to love me and approve of me."

CHAPTER 10

DEBRA'S WELCOME PARTY

Be gracious to me, O Lord, for I am languishing; heal me, O Lord, for my bones are troubled.

—PSALMS 6:2 (ESV)

A WELCOME HOME PARTY

The night I dreaded was upon me. After work, I made dinner and cleaned the kitchen. I was in no hurry to get to Debra's party. For the past week, I had beat myself up for agreeing to go. I knew this was wrong on so many different levels.

The wind was blowing, and it was cold outside. But that didn't stop me from walking so slowly. For the first time, I was way behind Scott and Austin. T.J. ran to the building and yelled, "Mom, hurry, I'm freezing."

With sadness in my heart, I turned to Scott and said, "I'm sorry. I must do this for Polly. Just a brief appearance, and we can leave."

When I walked into the nursing home, streamers, balloons, and banners hung high on the walls. The signs read: "It's a Girl" and "Our Family Is Finally Complete." Instantly, I didn't feel welcomed. I knew I needed to find somewhere I could hide inconspicuously. Scott whispered in my ear, "I got this," as he held Austin. "Stay right behind me, keep your head down, and I'll run interference."

I almost cracked up. He was talking like this was a football game, but I did exactly as he said as I looked down at the floor. Scott suddenly stopped, and I ran smack into him. Hesitantly, I looked up, and Bill was next to me. He must have seen the terror on my face. "Hi, Shirl," he said. "You'll be fine. Mom and Debra are in Dad's room."

My body trembled as I hugged Bill. "Thanks."

I followed Scott to an alcove down the hall opposite James's room. I was able to watch without being seen. I was glancing around the lobby area. I saw aunts, uncles, cousins, and family friends. I was terrified to visit with them. I was worried Hilda might have said derogatory things about me. To my utter horror, someone was videotaping the occasion. Nudging Scott, I said, "We need to move back there. I don't want to be in the video."

I was watching this joyous celebration unfold for Debra. It was more than my heart could handle. I had returned to my past, lurking in the shadows, not belonging, and feeling ashamed. I was again the deep dark secret hidden away. My mom Polly didn't want to meet me, much less celebrate her newfound daughter. All I wanted to do was run and hide.

The room broke out in a commotion. Suddenly, Debra and Jean walked out of James's room. I think my jaw must have dropped. Debra didn't resemble the photo I had seen. There was a tall woman with bright red hair. Her makeup was applied quite liberally, and her face was bright red, like her lipstick. Her dress caught my eye. It was maroon, sleeveless, and made of crepe. She was wearing open-toed strapped stilettos, necklaces, and bracelets.

When I heard her speak, I was in shock. Her voice was exactly like the Morgan sisters. I quietly said, "Undoubtedly, she is one of them. I don't belong here. I feel like an uninvited guest. We need to leave now."

I had never seen Scott move so quickly. I was behind him, again, my shield. Then, I heard a booming voice say, "We need a picture of Shirley and Debra together."

I felt my dinner in my throat. No way did I want to pose for a picture. The video camera was more than enough. Scott stopped, and with force, I ran into him. He was shoving me forward, and I slowly walked up.

I was about five feet from her when I smelled alcohol. I stood beside her, and she hugged me. The smell of alcohol overpowered me. As soon as the picture was taken,

I made a beeline for the door. Jean grabbed my arm and said, "Dad wants to talk to you."

With all eyes on me, I had no choice. Scott had to push me into James's room. James was all covered up in his bed. He looked at me, and without displaying any emotion, he said, "You're still my daughter."

What brought this on? Displaying a loving and perfect Cleaver family for the camera. He wanted me to hug him, which I begrudgingly did. Seething, I said, "Sure. It's time for us to leave."

We quickly exited his room, not looking back. I broke out from Scott's grip and ran for the front exit. T.J. and Scott were following me.

We all got in the truck. My head was spinning, and my heart was pounding. I was out of breath, and my body was shaking. All I wanted was to go home.

THE PSYCHIATRIC WARD
A couple of days later, my Aunt Mary called. I was excited to speak with her. She sounded upset and talked fast. "Debbie is in the hospital. Tomorrow, Polly is flying into Billings, Montana. I'm picking her up at the airport. And then we'll drive to Gillette."

I peppered her with questions. What happened? Did she have an accident? Is she going to be okay? When I finally stopped with the questions. Aunt Mary sounded worse. I heard her take a deep breath. She said, "All Polly said was that Debbie had a nervous breakdown and was hospitalized. I need to pack and get ready. I'll see you tomorrow."

I couldn't sleep that night. The agony I endured from the party rushed through my head. But tomorrow would be a new, glorious day since I was meeting my mom Polly for the first time ever. I prayed, "God, please be with them as they travel. I pray my mom Polly will love me. Amen."

In the morning, I took extra time getting ready, perfecting my hair and makeup. I wanted to look my best for Polly. I had to work until noon. All of my coworkers at the office were congregated around the coffee pot.

Excitedly I said, "You aren't going to believe this. My mom Polly is coming to Gillette with my Aunt Mary. Debbie has been hospitalized, and Polly is coming to see her."

I was busy, and before I knew it, the clock hit noon. Not long after I got home, my phone rang. Aunt Mary needed directions to my house.

I saw a car pull up in front and peeked out my window, feeling like a little kid waiting for the ice cream truck on a hot summer day. I couldn't wait and quickly ran outside to greet Aunt Mary and Polly. This was the moment I had been waiting for. I would finally get to look into the eyes of the mother who gave birth to me. I wanted to feel her arms embrace me and tell me she was happy to meet me and loved me.

I looked at my mom, taking her all in. She was a little taller than Aunt Mary, with broad shoulders, brown hair, and hazel eyes. This was surreal. My mom was here, and I could reach out and touch her. I walked up to her and hugged her with everything in me, trying to make up for all we had missed.

Standing: Polly and Shirley
Sitting: Aunt Mary and Grandson John – 2003

I could feel Polly's body tense up, and I had to let go of her. Smiling, I said, "You don't know how it feels to meet you finally."

Polly wasn't responsive at first. "Well," she said, "I'm glad to meet you."

I invited them into my house and hugged Aunt Mary. "I'm happy to see you again," I told her.

An uncomfortable silence enveloped the room until Aunt Mary filled it. "Why don't you show us your house," she said.

I apologized. "My mind was wandering," I said, "I'm sorry." I showed them around.

Scott stopped by to meet Polly and Aunt Mary. I watched Polly, and I could sense she was ready to leave. I wanted more time with her. One hour wasn't enough. Reluctantly, I asked, "Did you want to leave now?"

Polly, without hesitation, said, "I think it would be best if we went to the hospital. I want to check on Debbie."

Aunt Mary saw my look of distress. "Shirley," she said, "why don't you drive to the hospital, and we can follow behind you?"

"Sure," I said. "Just follow me."

I wanted to cry. This was not the reunion I had dreamed about. Polly's only concern was getting to the hospital to see Debbie. I could understand that, but it didn't lessen my hurt.

We arrived at the hospital and took the elevator to the fifth floor. A sign by the locked doors said we were required to notify the hospital staff whom we were visiting. As the doors slowly opened, a nurse was waiting for us. We showed her our driver's licenses and followed her. She unlocked the door to Debbie's room. I was the last one to enter.

Debbie was sitting in her hospital bed. She beamed with delight when she saw Polly. From there, it went downhill. Debbie spoke animatedly, almost childlike. "I met my mommy and daddy," she said. "They had a big party for me. My brothers and sisters were there to meet me. And a whole bunch of other people were there. I went home with Mommy because Daddy lives in the nursing home. Mommy's house was so pretty, and I loved it."

It was like listening to a six-year-old child. I felt terrible for Polly. I would be hurt if I were in her place. Polly tried to interject, "We just left Shirley's house. It was nice with three levels and a nice big backyard."

This conversation had turned into a competition, and I was appalled. Debbie was rubbing Polly's nose in her new life and family. My heart went out to Polly as she listened to her daughter exclaim how much better her new family was.

After that, I zoned out. My mind rushed with a flurry of thoughts. What in the world was happening? We only stayed about thirty minutes before the nurse came in to tell us our time was up. I was relieved.

As we left the hospital, I was hoping Polly would want to spend more time with me, but that wasn't the case. We went our separate ways, and I went home alone. I learned later on that Polly stayed in Gillette for a few days, but I never saw her again.

That evening, as I was finishing dinner, Scott dropped by. "I couldn't believe the three of you," Scott said. "Your mannerisms, the way you stand, walk, and carry yourselves are all the same. The only real difference is your voices."

CHAPTER 11

PATERNAL FAMILY

Whoever hates me hates my Father also.

—JOHN 15:23 (ESV)

THE AFTERMATH

After I made it home from the disastrous meeting and
hospital visit, I was inconsolable. Scott tried to make me
feel better, but I had so many emotions. I felt lost, abandoned, lonely, hopeless, heartbroken, and embarrassed.

Scott smiled. "I know what you need to do. Leave on a
Friday night for a weekend, and visit Aunt Mary. She
wants you to meet your cousins. If you want, Austin and
I will come with you. You need it after tonight, and it will
make you feel better."

I knew Scott was right. I prayed, "God, please help me.
I feel like I'm dying inside. I need your comfort. Amen."

The next day was beautiful, and the cool crisp air reminded me winter was coming. Austin cooperated as I dropped him off at day care and went to work. I said a quick prayer for strength before I got out of my car.

I opted out of the morning coffee pot social with my coworkers. Instead, I sat at my desk. The girls came into my office. They asked, "Soooo, how did it go meeting your mother?"

With that question, I lost it. There were tears and hugs all around. After telling them the reunion with Polly wasn't what I had hoped for, they showered me with compassion and understanding.

Feeling much better, I said, "You are so wonderful, and I appreciate each of you. Thanks for always listening to me. I try to keep my feelings hidden, but sometimes they bubble up, and I lose control."

A few weeks later, I began making plans for my visit to Worland. I phoned Aunt Mary and said, "Scott, Austin, and I are planning a trip to Worland. What weekend works best for you? I want to spend more time there and meet my cousins."

Aunt Mary said, "What about next weekend? I'm sure we will all be home."

Excited, I responded, "Friday, I could leave work early, and we could return on Sunday."

We ended our call after our plans were set. I was thrilled and couldn't wait to leave. The days were passing by quickly. On Thursday after work, I went to Scott's to pick up Austin. I asked, "Scott, are you packed? I can't wait to leave tomorrow."

Scott said, "Yep, we are all packed. Aren't we, Austin? He wanted a few toys from here."

Austin snuggled into Scott. "My 'cott, Nana." That was his nickname since he couldn't say Scott.

The following day, we were packed and on our way. After we arrived, Scott was coughing, "Shirl, I'm going to stay at the hotel. I don't feel very good. Austin can stay with me, and you can visit without interruptions."

I looked at them. Scott was under the covers. Austin was hanging on to his moose and snuggled beside Scott, "Bye, you be a good boy," I said to Austin. "I love you guys."

Aunt Mary and I drove around Worland, and she showed me where my cousins and relatives lived. We ended up at my cousin Nick's house. I had never met him before. He approached me and embraced me. "Welcome to the family," he said. "This is my wife, Brenda, and we have a son and two daughters."

Looking around, I could tell he loved to hunt. He had elk and deer mounted on his walls. A wood stove was crackling in the corner. Nick reminded me of my brother

Bill, only a foot shorter. They both had a sense of humor. Brenda was half-Mexican, like me. She was the kindest person, and I was in awe. How could I feel such an instant connection to them? I felt like I had known them forever. It must be in our genetics.

I listened to stories of my grandmother, who had passed away. And we talked about our cousin Kim and her sister. I knew that Aunt Mary, Nick, and Brenda were close. Brenda said, "Aunt Mary and I go to lunch once a week."

Nick made fun of me, saying, "You're just a little Chicana."

I still needed to learn what that meant. I said, "Okay, you need to explain that. I have no idea what that means. I never took Spanish in school."

I made him laugh hard. "A Chicana is a Mexican woman born in the United States," he said.

It was getting late. "I probably should be leaving here in a few minutes," I said. "Scott isn't feeling well, and Austin is with him."

We said our goodbyes. Aunt Mary and I made our plans for the next day. I was going with the flow, which was unusual because I was typically a planner. But I thought, *Let go, let God.*

The next day Austin came with me. We went to my cousin Kim's store. As we walked in, I saw her waiting for us. She looked cute in her denim bib overalls. Her skin was fair, almost porcelain, against her jet-black hair and brown eyes. Not as tall as me, but we could have been sisters. Aunt Mary took our picture.

Kim had an eye for decorating, and it was beautiful. Her store smelled like the fresh flowers she sold. I took everything in. Books and decorative pieces sat on the shelves throughout the store. Austin found the kid's corner. He sat at a small table and played with a train set. Aunt Mary exclaimed, "I can't believe how blond his hair is and those blue eyes."

I smiled. "My children all had blond hair as toddlers. Chris is the male version of me but with dark green eyes. Lindsay's hair is light brown, but she colors it black, like my natural color. Her eyes are a dark hazel brown. T.J.'s hair is light brown, and his eyes are hazel with blue."

It felt so good to talk about my children. Polly hadn't inquired about my children. It hurt my feelings, but she was consumed with Debbie's health. I sat with Aunt Mary and Kim for hours. It was a repeat of the night before, and I felt we had always known each other. We went to lunch together.

Kim said, "I have a son who will graduate from high school in two years. I don't know if Mom told you, but I had him when I was young and unmarried. When I went to college, my parents took care of him."

I nodded. "I had my son Chris when I was eighteen," I said. "My parents and I weren't close before. But my parents and sister Hilda supported me during my pregnancy. They helped me raise Chris for over two years. Isn't it crazy? Not only do we look alike, but we have endured similar events in our lives."

After lunch, I checked on Scott, and he was feeling miserable. "I think it would be a good idea if we went home," I said. "I don't want you to lie in a hotel room when you could be home."

Our visit was cut short, but I enjoyed myself. My relationship with Aunt Mary, Kim, Brenda, and Nick flourished. I knew I could pick up the phone anytime, and they would be there for me just as I would be for them. I told everyone goodbye and promised I would be back soon.

MY FATHER'S NAME

Polly and I had phone conversations at least once every two weeks. The calls were superficial. Polly wasn't forthcoming about my new family, even after several phone calls and a visit with her. I still knew nothing about my biological father. With all the courage I could muster, I asked, "What is my father's name?"

She said, "His nickname was D.C., and he was from Arvada, Wyoming. The last I knew, he had five kids. But I heard he had passed away in maybe 1988."

I was surprised she was forthcoming. I had called Aunt Mary recently, and I was frustrated. No matter what I did or how hard I tried, Polly kept me at an arm's distance. She didn't want a relationship with me, which broke my heart.

Aunt Mary said, "I'm so sorry for you, and I don't know what to tell you. Your mother is like that. She doesn't talk to me about her family. I have to pry information from her."

I was grieving for a father I would never meet. The hospital's error had taken him from me, too. I wanted to see him, touch him, and watch his mannerisms. I resembled Polly, but my physical build was different, maybe like my father's.

Once again, I went into private investigator mode. I started searching for information about my paternal siblings. A group of my girlfriends who were familiar with public records searches helped out, too.

My best friend Diane located my father's obituary. "Hey, Shirl, we have information about your father. I'm going to fax it to your office now."

I ran to the fax machine. I grabbed the papers and returned to my office. I read them at my desk, and my hands trembled as I read D.C.'s obituary. Only five short paragraphs long. He died on November 29, 1987, and his wife and children were listed. There was no photo. The following page was "Record of Funeral," which had a wealth of information about his life. He had served in the military and was a mechanic. His parents' names were listed. I had a half sister named Lynda, and in 1987, she lived in Gillette. What were the chances she still lived here?

I couldn't wrap my head around that fact. My half sister could still live in Gillette. I checked the phone book, but her name wasn't in it. Then I had a light bulb moment; my brother-in-law had grown up around the same area. There was a good chance he might know her. He knew everyone. I called him right away. My hunch was correct.

He said, "Shirl, I know her. I'll do some digging and call you right back."

REJECTION

Within the hour, I had her number. I was a bundle of nerves as I paced back and forth. I prayed Lynda would accept me and want to talk to me. I didn't think I had the strength to handle another rejection.

I dialed the number, taking silent deep breaths as it rang. When she answered, I said, "Hello, this is Shirley Larsen. I recently discovered I had been switched at birth. I'm not sure if you have heard anything about it?"

I paused, but she didn't say a word. I didn't know what to make of it. Did I jump right in and tell her? Was there a proper way to say this? I forged ahead. "I discovered my biological father's name, and I would really..."

Lynda kept me from finishing. Rudely, she shouted, "Yes, I have. We do not want anything to do with you. This story has been all over the media. Our family wants privacy. Don't ever contact me or anyone in my family."

I pleaded with her, "I haven't spoken to the media. The Morgan family are the ones talking to the media. Would you please talk..."

Lynda slammed the phone down before I could finish.

The sorrow and self-doubt seeped in. What was wrong with me? How could this happen again? Why was I being rejected at every turn? Lynda had never spoken to me and certainly didn't know me. How could she be so cruel?

After a lifetime of rejection, I was heartbroken.

A week later, I called Polly. We began with small talk. I eventually told Polly about the conversation I had had with my half sister. I was embarrassed.

Polly wasn't surprised. She said, "Debbie called her father, D.C., sometime around 1988. His wife answered the phone and told her D.C. was dead and to never call again. They wanted nothing to do with her."

Polly went on to explain her relationship with my father. "When D.C. and I were dating, he introduced me to his parents. They didn't like me because I was Mexican. After Debbie was born, D.C. used to come over to see her. His parents wanted to adopt Debbie, and I refused. Then, he got married. His wife was jealous of me, and he never returned to see Debbie again."

I wish I had known that before I called Lynda. It made sense that his family wanted nothing to do with Debbie or me. Their mom was jealous of something that happened forty-three years ago. And I was paying the price.

CHAPTER 12

MEDIA FRENZY

For you formed my inward parts; you knitted me together in my mother's womb. I praise you, for I am fearfully and wonderfully made.

—PSALM 139:13–14 (ESV)

MEDIA FRENZY

Scott invited us to Disneyland for Thanksgiving 2001. This was a tradition with his daughters, Jen and Leah. T.J. was spending the holiday with his dad. I wanted to take Austin to the pediatrician before we left. The pediatrician had seen him for his cough two weeks before, but the medication hadn't worked. That day, she changed his medications and assured me he would return to normal in a few days.

Scott was bathing Austin, and I was packing. The phone rang, and I ran down the stairs. "Hello, is this Shirley Larsen? I'm with the *National Enquirer...*"

I didn't let her finish and I didn't even catch her name. I hung up on her and was mad she had wasted my time. "Scott," I called out, "some lady said she was with the *National Enquirer*, and I hung up on her."

Scott and I laughed as I continued packing for our trip. Bright and early, we drove two hours to the airport. We arrived in Los Angeles later that evening. While everyone had fun on the trip, Austin's condition worsened, and we needed to get home and get him to the doctor.

The very next morning, after returning from Los Angeles, Diane called. I wasn't even out of bed yet. "Shirl, you aren't going to believe what was on the front page of the Sunday newspaper. A big picture of James in his bed at the nursing home with Jean beside him. You need to read it for yourself."

I said, "My attorney John told me the newspaper would be running the story. They had contacted John and asked if I would comment or be interviewed, but I declined."

Diane couldn't help herself. She started to tell me more about the article anyway. With sarcasm in her voice, she said, "The Morgans went on about how they didn't throw you away. They still loved you and always had. What a crock. They didn't love you before and don't love you now. It made me sick. The main part of the story was about what a miracle it was they found their daughter. They went on about the celebration they held for Debra. The article said the Morgan children thought of you as their sister. Oh, and there is a picture and article about the intermediary who saved the day" (McKay 2002).

"Are you kidding me?" I said. "The Morgans were allowed to share and talk about everything in the newspaper?"

A NEW YEAR

The new year 2002 was off to a terrible start after a month of doctor appointments and tests for Austin in Denver. We had a diagnosis. Austin had a bacterial infection in his lungs. The doctor wanted to hospitalize him, but I refused. I would care for him at home. I was so over-whelmed caring for Austin that I didn't have time to worry or think about what was happening around me. God knew I needed a break from all of the insanity.

I went to work at six o'clock in the morning. I was exhausted. I was able to schedule my work around Austin's IV treatments. A friend came into my office that morning and looked at me, "Shirl, you look like hell."

That made me laugh. I replied, "I probably look better than I feel. I'm a zombie, lucky to get four or five hours of sleep each night. The IV treatments are so time-consuming. I don't know how much longer I can do it."

On Feb. 12, 2002, Austin was hospitalized. The doctor said he would be released in two or three days if his blood work was good. He was put in an isolation room, and I stayed with him.

At lunch the next day, I heard the door open, waking me up. Scott was standing in the room with a massive stack of newspapers in his arms. He looked mad. He had a frown on his face, and his eyes were filled with rage. I knew whatever he had in his arms meant bad news. I squeezed Austin tightly to my chest, taking deep breaths and trying to prepare myself.

THE NATIONAL ENQUIRER

"Babe, I'm so sorry. I tried to buy as many copies as possible, but they are everywhere," he said.

I needed clarification. "Scott, what are you talking about?"

He picked it up, opened it, and handed it to me. The headline read, "Switched at Birth—and No One Knew for Forty-Three Years. One was a brown-eyed Hispanic, and one was a blue-eyed redhead."

The first thing I noticed was my photo in the upper left-hand corner. It was my sophomore class picture. The other photos were current and in vivid color. Photos of the Morgan family and my mom Polly (her photo was taken in her twenties) were splashed across the page. And mine was of a small old black-and-white photograph. My shoulders were rounded, I had a vacant stare, and I wasn't smiling (McKay 2002).

After reading the article, I wanted to curl up in a ball. I was mortified. Who in their right mind would grant an interview to the *National Enquirer*? Later, I discovered that Hilda and Debra were paid for their interview.

Slapping the paper down, I yelled, "Why do they keep running to the media? What happened to the statement Hilda made in her letter to the editor, 'Going public has been a hard decision as we are quite private people.'"

Scott tried to lighten the mood. He said, "Shirl, how many people do we know who read the *Enquirer*? None, correct?"

He was right, but I was mad. This was my life and my story to tell, but I couldn't. I was an emotional wreck. Every day that passed by, I found it hard to keep everything pushed down. I would need to grow a thicker skin because more was yet to come.

MY BIRTH

Polly moved to Worland in the spring of 2002, and I went to see her. After each visit, I walked away feeling empty. Polly wouldn't let me in her life. All I wanted was to be her daughter. Stubborn as I am, I would keep trying. When I was in Worland, I always stayed with Aunt Mary. Once, I called Polly, and she said she was working that day. She cared for elderly people in their homes. "Would one o'clock work for you?" she asked. "My patient will be taking her afternoon nap."

I hadn't met her husband, Juan. From all the stories I had heard about him, I wasn't looking forward to that meeting. Cheerfully, I replied, "Of course, I can't wait to see you."

I prayed, "Dear Lord, may this be the beginning of our relationship. Amen." I wanted to know more, especially about my birth. I only knew about Jean giving birth in the hallway. I read more information from the newspaper article. But I wanted to hear Polly tell her story. And this was a perfect time.

We started with small talk. I asked, "How is Jon doing?" He was my youngest half brother and the one sibling who accepted me from the start. He was a safe subject.

Polly answered, "Jon is busy working. I see him at night, cook dinner, and pack his lunch. But we don't have enough time to sit and talk like we used to."

Jon was her baby, and her life revolved around him. I could understand. I did the same thing with my children. My courage was built up. I said, "I would love to hear the story of my birth."

To my utter amazement, Polly began, "My contractions started during Easter Mass. They weren't too bad, and I slept all night. At lunch the next day, the contractions hurt and were closer together. I walked to the hospital."

My mouth dropped open. She acted like it was no big deal to be in labor and walk to the hospital. I would eventually drive the one-and-a-half-mile route, thinking about the story Polly told me about my birth. But I discovered important information she didn't tell me.

Before Easter 1958, there had been a snowstorm. All of the streets in Gillette were dirt. It had to have been a muddy mess. And she would have had to climb a big hill. All alone, in labor, and carrying a suitcase. It was hard for me to comprehend how strong Polly was.

"The only thing I remember is I started hemorrhaging and had blood transfusions," she continued. "The next thing I remember was the nurse bringing Debbie into my room for me to nurse her."

I knew the answer but asked, "What did your baby look like?"

Polly said, "Debbie had fair skin, hair, and eyes. I thought she looked like her father, D.C."

Our lovely visit abruptly halted when a Mexican man walked into the house. It was Juan. He was short, maybe five feet and a few inches. He was stocky, with brown eyes covered by glasses. He had dark, graying hair and a stoic look on his face. He shook my hand with a tight grip. His hands were enormous. He looked like Craig.

Juan looked at Polly and said, "I need to talk to you."

I knew it was time to leave. "It was nice visiting you," I said. "I hope to see you again before I leave."

Polly looked frightened. "I will be on my days off and at home," she said.

I took that as a sign. She was telling me, "Don't come over."

As I walked to the door, Juan's voice was raised, speaking Spanish. I was never so glad to get out of there.

Kim, my cousin, came over to her mom's. Aunt Mary made tacos, and the shells were homemade and deep-fried. We sat and talked and laughed the night away. I learned more about my other two aunts. My uncle was Nick's dad, who had died in a tragic automobile accident. I only heard and learned about my family through Aunt Mary. Kim and I had much in common, and I cherished my visits.

ACCUSATIONS

On Thursday, April 5, 2002, I was at work when an instant message popped up on my computer from my half brother Craig. I opened it up, and he said he had a question. I was surprised. I hadn't spoken to him since our October visit.

Craig started with a recitation of outlandish accusations. "I heard you told people how disappointed you were with my mom. Is that true?"

I tried to explain, "I was happy to meet Polly. I have done nothing to warrant your accusations. I have no idea what you're talking about. Where did you hear this?"

Craig said he heard that through the grapevine. He said, "I love my mother and will not let anything hurt her. I have the resources to protect her from you. I have your number and will call you this evening."

I was stunned. Why would he say those things? I only wanted a relationship with my mother, Polly.

Craig never called me again, but all my insecurities came creeping in. Would he say something to Polly?

That was the last communication I had with him.

I desperately wanted Polly to love me. I would never hurt Polly or take advantage of her. What was I going to do? How could I prevent this from happening? I turned to God and prayed, "Please grant me a relationship with my mother. Amen."

On April 8, 2002, I received my first birthday card from Polly. It read: "Sure is nice to have you as my daughter, even though I just found you or you found me, I should say. We have so much to learn about each other and the family. But I am glad we are together. It sure feels good. I hope you had a nice birthday. All my love, Your Mother."

I was ecstatic to read this card after what Craig had said to me. This gave me hope. But I still had a niggling feeling in the back of my head. Did she mean what she had written? Because up until then, she hadn't acted that way.

On April 12, 2002, Hilda, Vicky, and Debbie appeared on the CBS *Early Morning Show*. They were flown to New York City to share Debbie's story of being switched at birth. Jean mentioned they were going to be on national news, and she said she would record it and give me a copy.

But I couldn't wait for the recording. I wanted to watch it live and see what they had to say. I was getting ready for work when they came on the television screen. They sounded and looked like triplets. They were all giggling as sisters should and acting silly. They kept touching one another, and there was no doubt they were sisters. I watched the short interview and went about my day.

POLLY'S DECISION

Polly called me a week later. I didn't have a chance to visit her before I left Worland. She declined our invitation to go out for dinner while I was visiting Aunt Mary and Kim. I thought she called to talk about the CBS *Morning Show*.

She made small talk, and I said, "Thank you for the birthday card. I loved it, and it made my day."

Polly said, "Well, I'm glad you liked it."

This would be an opportune time to talk more about my children. I had never gone into detail about them, and she never asked about them. As I started talking about my children, I could sense Polly wasn't paying attention.

She just kept responding, "Oh, that's nice."

It was crushing to me that Polly didn't seem to care about her grandchildren or making up for lost time. She never acknowledged them on birthdays or Christmas.

Then Polly made it clear the real reason for her call. "How is your lawsuit against the hospital going? I'm so mad at the hospital. It has ruined my life. It's their fault the media is talking about me like I was just some unwed Mexican. I don't understand how the hospital could switch two babies. I'm thinking about suing the hospital."

I had never seen this side of her, and I wasn't about to interrupt her.

Polly continued, "I want to file a lawsuit against Banner Health. Juan told me I could. But I don't know any attorneys. Could you help me?"

This was the first time Polly asked me for help. When she told me Juan was pushing her to file a lawsuit, I knew he must rule her with an iron fist. I said, "Of course, I'm happy to help you. Would it be okay if I ask my attorney John for a recommendation?"

Polly replied, "That would be fine with me."

I was excited she wanted my help, and I immediately called John. "Polly wants to file a lawsuit," I told him. "She doesn't know attorneys. This is the first time she has asked me for help, and I'm overjoyed. Would you please help me?"

John said, "Yes, absolutely. I'll email you a list of attorneys. But I know one here in Casper, and he is great. I'll give you his information right now."

I called Polly back and told her, "I have a name and contact information for a good attorney in Casper."

"Thank you," she said. "I'm going to call him right now."

Polly hired him, and our cases were combined. For the first time, I felt like I was Polly's daughter, lending her a helping hand when she needed it most. We were in this together.

CHAPTER 13

ROSIE MAGAZINE

But if you have bitter jealousy and selfish ambition in your hearts, do not boast and be false to the truth.

—JAMES 3:14 (ESV)

ANOTHER WELCOME PARTY

Scott, Austin, and I were outside enjoying the beautiful summer weather. The mailman pulled up, and I ran to meet him. He handed me a stack of mail that I sorted. I found a small card from Jean.

When I opened the card, a clipping from the newspaper dropped out with an ad that Jean had placed in the newspaper, announcing a community-wide celebration for Debra. Jean was hosting another party and expected me to show up.

They could have as many parties as they wanted, but why did Jean keep inviting me? Didn't she know how much it hurt me? I threw the card at Scott and went inside. I felt like the wind had been knocked out of me.

I wasn't going to feel sorry for myself. I was going to enjoy the family God had blessed me with. Smiling, I said, "Scott, let's have a barbecue tonight and watch a movie. We need to do something."

Several uneventful weeks passed by. It was Sunday, June 16—a week after Debra's party. Chris called me as I was getting ready for church, asking, "Are you and T.J. going to the nursing home? I'll meet you there."

Darn it, I didn't want to, but I had to go for my sons. James and Jean were still their favorite grandparents. After church, we went to the nursing home. While they visited, I took Austin on a walk.

When we returned to James's room, Jean handed me a bag and said, "These are for you from Debra's party. We missed seeing you there."

What, why was she giving me Debra's cards? I shrugged, "Oh, thanks."

When I got home, I put the cards in my files without opening them. When was this going to stop? Was Jean doing these things to me out of anger or insensitivity?

US DISTRICT COURT HEARING
On September 19, 2002, our case was to be heard. Our attorneys told Polly and me we didn't need to appear, but we both wanted to go. When I walked into the courtroom, it was intimidating. The floors were marble, beautiful

woodwork adorned on the walls, and the table would seat thirty or forty people.

When the judge came in, the court was in session.

Polly and I both had our backs straight. I knew Polly was terrified. I kept my face emotionless as I said a silent prayer.

The judge began, "I want you to focus on the unique issue and the sufficiency of the pleading on the claim for emotional distress."

I listened to endless back-and-forth debating between the attorneys. "If you assume they were switched at birth, and it was the hospital's fault..." Banner Health's attorney said. Banner Health operated the hospital in 1958 and denied all responsibility.

The judge was not having any of that. "There's no proof required in this case. Is there?" he said. "Look at the negligence in and of itself. There's egregious negligence here. Wouldn't you agree?"

Thank you, God. The judge seemed to be on our side. He wasn't putting up with Banner's outlandish theories and denials.

The judge addressed the notion of emotional damages. "Is that all we're dealing with here, emotional damages? I wonder if any of us in this room, switched in our cradles taken from our mothers, advised forty years later of the mistake, would look at this as just negligence."

The judge then said, "I think in deference to my colleagues on the Supreme Court of Wyoming, I want to let them have an opportunity to see whether yet another refinement of the current state of law should be permitted in cases such as this because, very candidly, there is no case such as this. Two children robbed of their identity forty-four years ago are now in this court. I will not base it on a cold-blooded interpretation and dismiss this cause of action. If I were making the law, I would carve out an exception and allow this matter to go forward."

After the attorneys' allotted time was up, the hearing was over. With compassion, the judge said, "Ms. Larsen and Ms. Polly Leyva, I don't know how this will turn out. I will never see you again if it doesn't turn out how you would like. In this courtroom, I want you to know personally how sorry I am that you have been subjected to this horrible torment."

ROSIE MAGAZINE ARTICLE

I started receiving phone calls from Martha Barnette, a freelance writer. My attorney John was fielding the media requests. I wondered how she got my phone number. I was sick of it, and for a while, I quit answering my phone.

A few weeks later, the freelance writer called again. I was vulnerable and let down my guard. I began listening to Martha. "This conversation is off the record. I know this is hard for you. Without your interview, the magazine article won't be complete. Are you sure?"

I said, "I'm not ready emotionally. I'm sorry, but I have to decline."

Martha continued, "What about having a friend do the interview for you? Would you be willing to let them talk for you? Hilda told me you never talk to each other, and she didn't understand the problem. But I know there is far more to this story."

After she said that, I started thinking, *I guess I could ask my best friend Diane if she would be willing. I'll call her tomorrow and ask her.* "You can call me tomorrow, and I'll have an answer for you."

When I called Diane, she jumped. "Yes, I will. I want people to hear your story."

After many calls and emails between Diane and Martha, the article was scheduled to be published in the November 2002 *Rosie Magazine.* The day the magazine hit the stands, I bought extra copies. I rushed home and began searching through the magazine for the article. It was titled "The Lost Daughters." The first page had Debbie's baby picture, and I was a year old in mine. On the other side was a picture of Hilda and Debbie. Their faces were cheek to cheek, each with a big smile.

I began reading the article. It was well-written, and I learned things I didn't know.

The article read: "Tales of babies switched at birth are almost as old as time itself. King Solomon settled a dispute after a mother intentionally swapped her own baby with another." I was intrigued and wanted to know more. Looking in my Bible, I found the story in 1 Kings 3:16–28.

The article went on: "Cases like these strike at the heart of what it means to be a family, and they raise profound questions about how much of our personality depends on upbringing and how much depends on our genes. And they speak to our primal fears and vulnerabilities" (Barnette 2002).

Debra talked about her difficult life in the article. She married at seventeen and later divorced. She attended college for two years and worked in various secretarial offices. She moved to Arizona in her thirties and lived in a public park, sleeping in a stairwell and public restrooms. Then she went to work as a secretary for a brokerage firm.

"I wish I could have been carried by my daddy just once," Debra was quoted in the article. "Who would I have been if I had grown up with my rightful family?" (Barnette 2002).

Days after the magazine was published, I stopped by the salon. Diane was on the phone shouting, "I'm glad Shirl found out, and I can't believe she could survive living in the Morgan family. And don't you ever contact me again."

I knew it had to be Vicky on the phone. I began apologizing, "Diane, I am so sorry I put you in that position. I had no idea that Vicky would call you."

Diane said, "When I answered the phone, she yelled, 'Are you Diane?' So you did the interview for the *Rosie Magazine*?'"

Still screaming, Vicky went on to say, "You had no right to do that. You don't know us. And how long have you known Shirley?'"

Diane rubbed my arm as she said, "I tried to cut in and explain how well I did know you, but she wouldn't allow it. She didn't want to hear anything I had to say. She repeatedly said, 'Shirley has always been nothing but a spoiled rotten brat. If you knew Shirley, you would at least know that about her. If you were smart, you would stay the hell away from Shirley.'"

I had never seen Diane this angry. She shook her head at me and said, "I don't know how you made it out of that family intact?"

My head dropped into my hands, embarrassed and ashamed. "I'm so sorry. I had no idea there would be repercussions to that interview. I promise you I'll never put you in that position again."

FIRST THANKSGIVING

Polly called a couple of weeks after the magazine was published. "Shirley," she asked, "would you and your family want to come to Worland and spend Thanksgiving with us? I haven't told you yet, but Craig has disowned us and wants no further contact."

Oh my gosh, I couldn't believe Craig had done that to her. But I was thrilled about the invitation and said, "I don't believe we have any plans this year. We would love to come. I'll call you back as soon as I know for sure. And I'm sorry about what Craig has done."

After I hung up, I felt like dancing. This would be my first holiday with my mom Polly. I knew in my heart the guys would be up for it. That evening, I asked the guys if we could go to Worland for Thanksgiving. T.J. said, "It's fine with me, but you'll need to call Chris."

Scott said he would ask his daughter Leah, too.

I was hesitant to call Chris. He hadn't even met Polly, and I felt like I was putting him in a difficult situation because he was so close to his grandma Jean. Of all my kids, Chris was the closest to his grandparents.

I called him anyway. "Chris, Polly invited us to Worland for Thanksgiving. Would you like to come?"

Without hesitation, he said, "No, I already have plans, but thanks for asking."

I understood and didn't expect him to come. Later, Scott called. "Leah said she would love to go."

I called Polly, excited. "Hi, we will be there for Thanksgiving Day," I said. "What would you like me to bring?"

Polly sounded happy. "You don't need to bring anything," she said. "Is it okay if I cook a Mexican dinner?"

Smiling, I said, "That would be awesome. I'll see you soon. Let me know if you need me to bring a dish or dessert."

Thanksgiving Day arrived, and I noticed T.J. was a little apprehensive. He had always been shy. Polly greeted us, and the aroma of Mexican food wafted through her house. Soon, Leah and Juan were deep in conversation, speaking Spanish. Leah had been studying Spanish for years.

My brother Jon was there, and he hugged me. "Hi, big sister," he said. "I'm glad you came."

I went into the kitchen to help Polly. She leaned close to me and said, "I settled my lawsuit. It was too hard for me. I was a nervous wreck. Juan has been mad because he will have to give a deposition."

I put my hand on her shoulder. "I understand," I said. "It's difficult for me. We make a little progress, and then we take two steps back. It will be a long process."

Aunt Mary's son, wife, and kids dropped by. I was happy to meet them. Austin played with their kids. Things were going great until Juan walked up to Austin and grabbed the toy out of his hands.

In a harsh tone, he said, "This is my toy, not yours."

Austin started crying, and Juan stood there with the toy still in his hand. "Hey, what's the big deal? I was kidding around. What is he crying for."

Juan had ruined the day, and the house went silent. My cousin's wife said, "We are leaving now."

She looked at me and said, "I will never bring my family here again. Juan is cruel, and he always has been. We wanted to come and visit with you and your family. I'm sorry, but we are leaving before it gets worse."

She said what I was thinking, and I began cleaning up the dishes. I felt terrible, but I wouldn't put up with Juan. He was beyond mean. Polly and I were in the kitchen.

I told her, "I'm sorry, but we need to leave. It's time for Austin's nap, and he can sleep in the car. Thank you for inviting us. The meal was delicious. And Leah enjoyed conversation in Spanish with Juan."

We got out of there as fast as we could. "I'm sorry," I told the kids. "I thought Juan would be nice for once."

T.J. said, "Mom, it wasn't your fault, but I'm never going back there."

CHAPTER 14

48 HOURS

He has told you, O man, what is good; and what does the Lord require of you but to do justice, and to love kindness, and to walk humbly with your God?

—MICAH 6:8 (ESV)

48 HOURS—DECEMBER 5, 2002

In June 2002, my attorney, John, called me, "Shirl, I received a letter from Erin Moriarty from *48 Hours*. I'll email you the letter. Are you interested?"

I replied, "No, I'm not, but I'll read it."

The letter read, "I am writing to ask whether you would be willing, at some point in time, to talk with me, either on or off-camera. I have moved slowly on this story because I recognize how life-changing this event has been for you. While the story of the baby switch has been portrayed in the newspapers and television as a happy event and reunion, the truth is far more complex and poignant. The fact that you have filed a lawsuit is an indication of the damage you suffered as a result of a careless and possibly negligent act of a hospital worker forty-four years ago. While I understand your desire for privacy at this time, I believe there is also a benefit for you and for others to speak publicly about what you are going through."

Even though I declined the interview, the program would still air without me.

A week later, my brother Bill called me. He said, "Shirl, you owe me big time. I met with the producer from *48 Hours*. She was beautiful and asked me to do an interview. And Shirl, I had to tell her no. I would only consider it if my sister Shirl sat beside me."

Bill made me cry. "You are so sweet," I told him. "Thanks. And I do owe you big. I will never forget this."

My little brother Bill had an unconditional love for me. I called Scott to tell him what Bill had said to me. Scott said, "Shirl, I know Bill has always been there for you. I bet he was laughing when he said it."

I smiled. "Yes, Bill was laughing."

On December 5, 2002, Chris, T.J., and I went to the family room to watch the *48 Hours* program. The network had been advertising the episode about my life for weeks. They called it "The Switch." I closed my shutters, and we all sat down on my long blue couch. The program began with video footage of Gillette. I was snuggled in, holding Austin. He was my source of comfort.

Bill and Shirley – 2022

I was surprised by a lot of Hilda's comments in the story. Some of the facts were stretched, and I was left shaking my head, wondering where she came up with this storyline. She took credit for ordering all of our DNA tests, and that was simply a lie.

But then I was shocked to learn on national television that Hilda was given medical records and knew my birth mother before I did.

On the show, host Erin Moriarty interviewed Hilda and talked about tracking down the official birth records. Hilda said she had to use distilled water and Clorox to uncover the names that were blacked out on the records. "We were desperate at this time," she said. "I soaked the paper for two full days." That's when she uncovered Polly's name (Klug 2002).

I was upset after hearing Hilda received official birth records from the hospital because I was told the hospital couldn't release any confidential information.

The *48 Hours* program praised the confidential intermediary who tracked down Debra in two and a half hours for the Morgan family. An intermediary can open birth records and even sealed adoption files in the state of Wyoming. This woman had read the Morgan's family editorial in the newspaper and started investigating on her own.

As I watched the show, I was grateful I declined the interview. As the twenty-eight-minute episode came to an end, all I could think about was moving forward. I didn't want to keep reliving my past.

Erin ended the show: "Not every investigation can have a happy ending, and sometimes the truth can be hard to hear. But for the people I've met tonight, that's almost beside the point for them and countless others seeking answers to their lives' mysteries. Simply knowing the truth is enough" (Klug 2002).

WYOMING SUPREME COURT—APRIL 2003

It was finally time for the supreme court to decide whether we could sue Banner Health for purely emotional damages.

The supreme court traveled throughout Wyoming for its hearings. It convened on April 17, 2003, in the Newcastle High School gymnasium. After hearing the oral arguments, the court would later decide if Wyoming would change the law.

I followed Scott down the aisle, looking straight ahead. We sat down. Scott leaned over and whispered, "Jean and Hilda are a few rows back."

My hands were sweating as I held them tightly folded on my lap. My heart was pounding. Knowing they were sitting behind me made me nervous. Why had they come? This hearing had nothing to do with them. I felt beads of sweat gathering on my face as I kept my eyes focused on the podium.

Banner Health reiterated the same argument. I had it memorized. I wanted to scream, "You took forty-three years from Polly and me. How can you not be responsible?"

My attorney John stepped up to the podium. He picked up a card Jean had sent me on March 7, 2003, inviting me to a birthday celebration for James and Debra, and read it aloud. "Dear Shirl, we'll have a potluck lunch on Saturday, March 15, at one o'clock at the nursing home for Dad and Deb's birthdays. You and the family are invited. I hope you'll come."

There was no mention of my birthday in Jean's card, and John wanted to show the court my pain. John said, "I don't think Jean sent the invitation to hurt Shirley, but it did."

There was an audible gasp from the audience. They understood a small part of my pain. The hearing ended after the oral arguments finished.

RETURN TO WHERE IT BEGAN
John, Scott, and I went to lunch after the hearing. We strategized about the next steps. John asked, "Do you know any nurses who worked in the hospital during 1958?"

I said, "Yes, I know two nurses still here, and I'm pretty sure they worked during that time."

John asked, "Could you call them and ask if they would be willing to speak with us? Do you know who owns the old hospital? It would be great if all of us could walk through the procedures they followed at childbirth."

Within a few days, we contacted the nurses and received permission to walk through the old hospital. It was now housing the community college. John and I met up with both of the nurses. I made introductions, and we discussed the switch. They both still couldn't believe it had happened. We drove over to the old hospital to take a tour.

As we walked into the hospital, it was surreal. We passed the admissions desk, where I worked in 1977, and the nurse's station. The nurses who came with us went over the procedures from the labor, delivery, and care after delivery. They explained, "Back then, the mothers were given Demerol during childbirth. Their babies were taken away, cleaned up, weighed, and measured. It could be a few hours later before the mothers saw their babies."

We walked down the hallway to the obstetrics ward and nursery. I used to walk down that hall on my work breaks to look in the nursery at the babies.

The delivery room looked like little had changed. Even the large green floor tiles were the same. I could picture Polly lying on the delivery table. She had several blood transfusions and was given Demerol four times when she was in the labor room.

We stood in the delivery room. The nurses pointed over to the right to a small room a little larger than a closet. "That was where the babies were weighed and measured. And supplies were kept over here to make the baby's identification bracelets, blue beads for a boy, and pink for a girl. We used a needle threaded with elastic to make lettered beads spelling out the mother's last name."

John asked, "Do you know how it could have happened?"

One of the nurses said, "Maybe Jean's chart had been left in the delivery room. In all of the commotion, the bracelet was made using the name on the chart, Morgan."

I asked, "Only two babies were born minutes apart. One was Mexican, and the other was White. The mistake should have been obvious when the babies were taken to their mothers. It was such a small hospital with only thirty-one beds. How was it that Jean and Polly never saw each other?"

The nurse quickly clarified, "In 1958, unwed mothers and their babies were segregated from married mothers and babies." We walked through a set of double doors, "The unwed mothers' rooms were on the right-hand side, and the nursery for their babies was on the left-hand side. The nursery was connected, and only the nurses saw all the babies."

I exclaimed, "A door separated Jean, Polly, Debbie, and me, and it changed our lives for forty-three years."

CHAPTER 15

LA FAMILIA

This is my commandment, that you love one another as I have loved you.

—JOHN 15:12 (ESV)

FRUSTRATION

Months had passed, and it was now late summer 2003. We still didn't have an answer from the court. I found it incredible that Banner Health denied all responsibility. How could they refute DNA tests? The error was theirs alone.

I hadn't heard from Polly for quite some time. I thought I'd call her tonight after work. Then, one of my friends came into my office and said, "Hey, Shirl, do you think your family would teach us how to make tamales?"

"That sounds like a good idea," I said. "I'll call Aunt Mary and ask her. And I'll let you know tomorrow."

I called Aunt Mary and asked her if a friend and I could come over and learn how to make tamales.

Aunt Mary said, "I haven't made any for years. Brenda makes them for Nick and would love to teach you how."

Within a few days, we had it all planned. I called Polly. "Hi, this is Shirley. A friend and I will be in Worland on Friday. Brenda is going to teach me how to make tamales. I would love it if you joined us."

Polly didn't even hesitate. "No, I can't," she said. "I'm taking care of Jon's daughter. But I would like it if you and your friend stayed with me Friday night."

"That would be wonderful." I was so excited and said, "I'll see you Friday night."

When we walked into Polly's house, it smelled wonderful. Polly had made dinner for us. It was delicious—green pork chili, refried beans, Mexican rice, and homemade tortillas. I said, "I wish I could make round tortillas. I have tried many times."

Polly replied, "If you made tortillas every day like me, yours would be round. Practice makes perfect. I'll see you in the morning."

In the morning, we finished getting ready. We walked into the kitchen, and Polly had made us Belgian waffles for breakfast. *How uncanny,* I thought. *I make them all the time for the kids.*

After we ate, I smiled and said, "Thank you for letting us stay with you. And your meals were wonderful. Please stop by Aunt Mary's if you have a minute today."

My friend thanked Polly profusely and exclaimed, "All I know is that was the best Mexican meal I've ever had."

At Aunt Mary's, we had so much fun. Brenda brought the meat she had prepared the day before. And it still took most of the day to make tamales. We talked as we cooked, and we had a blast. Nick stopped by, "Have you learned anything from Brenda? She is the best cook, and we need to make you more Mexican. You need to come more often. Brenda enjoys spending time with you."

I smiled and said, "I will. We had so much fun."

As we were getting ready to leave, Aunt Mary asked, "My cousin's son is getting married in Omaha, Nebraska, on October 4, 2003. Do you want to come with me? I asked Polly, but she said no."

"Yes, I do," I said, smiling. "I'll call you and let you know for sure."

I said a silent prayer. "Dear Lord, I thank you for this time I had with my mother. And I pray you will see us safely home. Amen."

ACKNOWLEDGMENT—OCTOBER 2003

Aunt Mary and I went to Nebraska. It was two days of driving, and we spent the entire drive talking about family. When we arrived, we went to a dimly lit restaurant with traditional Mexican decor. A mariachi band began playing traditional Mexican music. I had never heard one before, and I loved the music. The band even came over to our table and serenaded us.

The following day we had a late breakfast and went shopping. Aunt Mary suggested we take a quick nap, and I agreed. I woke up and began getting ready, "What time is the wedding?" I asked.

I looked over at her. She had the invitation in her hand. She exclaimed, "We are late. Hurry up."

We rushed to the church and were met by the bride and groom walking out. With a twinkle in her eye, Aunt Mary said, "At least we didn't miss the reception. You'll have fun there."

At the reception, the most incredible thing happened. My cousin, the groom's father, came over to our table. He took my hand and walked me to the dance floor. Then, he put his arm around me, and with the microphone in his hand, he announced, "We have a special guest, Shirley Larsen, our new cousin. Without going into much detail, after DNA tests, she has been looking for her family. Welcome to la familia."

I felt my lip trembling, and tears welled up. This was the first time I was introduced as "la familia." Polly had never introduced me to our extended family. But finally, being accepted into my real family, where I truly belonged, was marvelous. Aunt Mary, in essence, became a surrogate mother to me.

As time went on, the phone calls dwindled between Polly and me. When I called her, our conversations were superficial. I thought our relationship would improve after I had spent the night at her house, but I was wrong.

AN ANSWER AND A QUESTION

My attorney John called me with exciting news. "Shirl, on December 23, 2003, the Wyoming Supreme Court voted in the affirmative. A jury will hear your case. We are going to be busy. First, I'll schedule a pretrial conference. Then we will begin depositions, looking for expert witnesses, and I want to do a mock trial."

I was speechless. I couldn't believe a jury would actually hear my case. I wanted to jump for joy. It took me a minute to reply, "God answered my prayers. I am ready to tell the jury exactly how forty-three years of my life were taken from me."

The Wyoming Supreme Court's decision was a front-page story for all the Wyoming newspapers. My case was now in the Wyoming law books: Larsen vs. Banner Health Systems. I had set a precedent.

A tremendous burden had been lifted off my shoulders. Now, I can relax and enjoy life for a few weeks.

At home, beautiful Christmas music played. The tree was decorated, and the house smelled like balsam pine. I baked cookies, and the presents were wrapped under the tree. On Christmas morning, Chris came over, and we opened presents. Chris and T.J. put the toys together for Austin while he played with the boxes.

Then, we all went to Scott's house. He was preparing prime rib for our Christmas dinner. We gathered around the tree. Austin was excited to open more presents. I watched as they all opened gifts, and then Scott handed me a small square box. I opened it, and inside was a solitaire diamond engagement ring. Scott dropped to one knee, "Shirl, would you marry me?"

We all smiled as I said, "Yes, I would love to marry you."

This was perfect. Our children were there, and we weren't just marrying each other. We were blending two families into one.

MY DEPOSITION

John called, "Your deposition is scheduled for March 11, 2004. I want to prepare you."

He went over the basics and said, "I have a couple of things we need to talk about. We could have a deterrent in your case. You are a successful professional, well-groomed, single mom raising a son and grandson." John explained the opposing attorneys could use that against us.

He went on to say, "James, Jean, and Debra are filing a lawsuit against the hospital, and they hired the attorney who declined your case."

This infuriated me. I said, "I blazed the way, and we did all the work. And now the Morgans want to jump on the bandwagon."

John said, "I'm sorry I dropped all the bad news, but I want you to be prepared for it."

My deposition was on a chilly spring day. On my drive to the courthouse, I was nervous. I prayed, "God, please give me strength and guidance. Amen."

The room was small. A court reporter and at least four attorneys were present. The table was close to the wall, and a video camera sat on a tripod with wires everywhere. As I sat down, John leaned in and assured me, "You'll be fine. Just tell the truth."

I sat straight with my hands folded in my lap. I was dressed in a white shirt, blazer, and pants.

The first hours of the deposition were spent reviewing my case. Then came the questions. A few of them torqued me off. The hospital's attorney asked, "Do you positively know the hospital switched you?"

I thought, *Give me a break.* "No, I was a baby," I responded.

They continued, "What if a person came off the street into the nursery and, as a joke, switched the babies? Maybe one of the doctors could have switched the babies?"

I wanted to jump up and scream, "Seriously, you think that is plausible?" But I sat calmly without revealing any emotion. I had perfected this technique.

Then came the question John and I had discussed. The Banner Health attorney asked, "Did the Morgans raise you to be a law-abiding citizen?"

I said yes.

The attorney continued, "Being raised by the Morgan family. You've done pretty well for yourself. You are a single professional woman, raising a twenty-year-old and four-year-old son independently."

I swallowed my bile. "I am who I am, despite the Morgan family."

After six hours, my deposition was finally finished. I wasn't nervous, but I was glad it was over. As the weeks passed, I received a birthday card from Polly. She wrote, "You have a happy birthday. Love, Mother."

Months before our wedding, Polly and Aunt Mary warned me to watch out for Benita. I have heard this statement numerous times. I didn't want to deal with drama in my new family, so I decided not to invite Benita to the wedding.

Finally, it was April 24, 2004, and it was our wedding day. It was supposed to be small, but it grew to quite the celebration of about eighty. Polly and Jean and many family members and close friends celebrated with us. Chris and T.J. walked me down the aisle. My best friend Diane and Scott's friend stood up with us.

We had a reception at the golf course and honeymooned in Cancun. It was perfect. I felt in my heart this was a new beginning for us.

EXPERT WITNESSES

The first week of May 2004, I flew to Seattle to meet a forensic psychologist who was one of our expert witnesses. I talked with him for several hours. After reading his report, one part took me by surprise.

"Shirley and Polly's lives seemed to follow striking similarities. Shirley rescues and makes amends for her mother's loss of her and the rejection and abandonment of the Morgans. Unwed teen pregnancies and unhappy adult relationships. These were a fantastic replication of the dynamics of Shirley's life. She was given a chance to work through this trauma. With the adoption of Austin. This adoption, in no small way, is associated with the level of health she presents with today."

I had never looked at my life this way. I found it fascinating. It was something I had never considered.

Next, I read the nurse's documents.

"Morgan baby, born at 3:07 a.m., weighed 6 lb. 12 1/2 oz., 18 1/2" long. Muñoz baby, born at 3:31 a.m., weighed 6 lb.

8 oz., 18-1/2" long. When the babies were dismissed, Morgan's baby went home on April 10, 1958. She weighed 6 lb. 3 oz. The Muñoz baby went home on April 13, 1958. She weighed 6 lb. 10 oz."

"Newborn babies lose 5 percent to 10 percent of their birth weight within three to four days after birth. The Morgan baby lost 9 1/2 ounces, and the Muñoz baby gained 2 ounces in five days."

I later realized the babies were correctly identified at birth, according to information we learned from the nurses. The bracelets should have been made after the babies were weighed and measured. How could the switch have taken place?

MOCK TRIAL

The mock trial was at Casper College. I was called to the stand and sat down. I held my hands tightly in my lap as I looked out and made eye contact with each juror, and then asked God to be with me. As the questioning began, I slowly felt my shoulders relax. After the first few questions, I realized I could do this. I don't remember all questions, just the sense of peace that passed over me.

God had been with me. I answered each question truthfully. I thought of the old saying, "When you tell the truth, the truth will set you free." I wanted a jury trial, especially after Banner Health had continually denied responsibility. This would be my time to tell my story.

The next day, John sent me the mock trial summary. Most of the comments were positive. Jurors agreed I was strong, caring, and loving. I was overcoming the love I didn't receive as a child. Most importantly, Banner was at fault. The jury also viewed my being a successful professional and single mom as a positive attribute—the opposite of what John and I thought.

I was excited to tell T.J. the news. I said, "Guess what! The mock trial results came back, and they all agreed they would vote in my favor in a trial."

When T.J. looked at me, he frowned and looked sad as he said, "Mom, please don't go to trial."

I was shocked. "Why not?"

He was somber. "Mom, aren't you sick of the media and the horrible way you have been treated? I want it to end. Do you have to go to trial?"

Right then and there, I decided, "No, T.J., I don't have to, and I'm not going to. I can go into mediation, and none of it will be publicized. I understand how you feel, and I don't like it either."

He smiled and said, "Thanks, Mom. I love you."

I smiled through tears. "I love you, too." When my children were born, I promised them they would not have a childhood like mine.

CHAPTER 16

MEDIATION

Do not be deceived: Bad company ruins good morals.

—1 CORINTHIANS 15:33 (ESV)

In the first part of August, John called and said, "Your mediation had been scheduled for September 16, 2004." John then reviewed the fundamentals of mediation with me.

He said, "You'll need to write a brief statement describing how being switched at birth has affected you and then memorize the statement. Speaking from your heart is far more effective than reading from a paper. At some point during mediation, I'll have you speak to all of us."

The summer flew by, and Jen, T.J., and Leah were at college. The house was eerily quiet, with only Scott, Austin, and me at home. I adopted Austin back in 2003, and Scott adopted him in 2005.

John called me toward the end of August. He said, "Do you have your statement memorized?" I told him I did, and he continued, "I just found out James, Jean, and Debra settled their lawsuit. Now it's just you left."

On September 15, 2004, Scott and I drove to Casper, Wyoming. That evening, we had dinner with John. He ran through the process one final time, and he said to me, "This is what we have been waiting for. Are you ready?"

I confidently said, "I'm ready. I have memorized my statement, but it's in my purse just in case."

Scott and I were up early the next morning. It was going to be a magnificent fall day. I wanted to enjoy the weather and take a short walk. I began thinking about all of the changes in my life these past three years. My past feelings of not belonging now made sense, and I knew who I was. I had been blessed with Aunt Mary, Kim, Nick, and Brenda in my life. And the extended family I was raised with still loved me. Nothing would ever change the bond we had. I was thankful as I prayed, "Dear Lord, I give you thanks for all you have blessed me with. And I ask that you would be with me today. Amen."

I met Scott, and we followed John into a small conference room. It had no windows and was poorly lit. A long table was off to the side. After introductions were made, we sat down. I was at the head of the table. Scott and John were by me, Banner Health's three attorneys were at the other end, and the mediator was in the middle.

The atmosphere was more relaxed than a courtroom. I felt composed with my statement in my hand. I played with it during tense moments. The attorneys presented their briefs. John gave them a dollar amount I would settle for. And Banner Health would counter. This back and forth continued for a few hours. We were at a standstill.

The mediator called for a break. John nodded for me to follow him. We entered the lobby, and John said, "Shirl, we aren't making any headway. It's time for you to speak. Are you ready?"

Without hesitation, I said, "Yes, I am."

John and I looked over and saw Scott kicking the pop machine. One of the Banner Health attorneys was also watching Scott, smirking. I walked up to Scott and asked him what was wrong. Frustrated, he replied, "I can't believe it. This stupid machine just took my last quarter."

Digging in my purse, I handed him a quarter and said, "Here, use this quarter. You'll be fine."

It was hilarious that in such a tense moment, Scott was worried about a quarter and the pop machine. Scott could always find a way to bring levity to a situation.

Everyone returned and took their places. John stood up and said, "Shirley would like to speak now."

I remained seated, silently praying, and spoke passionately from my heart.

"I wanted to go to trial, so everyone would know what your mistake has done to me and taken from me. An error that you have continually denied. Then you can explain your wild theories: someone coming off the street playing a joke by switching two babies or the doctors switching the babies. How can you deny DNA tests?" Tears were now streaming down my face. "You took from me the ability to phone my mom when I needed her. Instead, you sent me home with this wonderful Cleaver family. Or that is what the Morgan family would love the public to believe. But we know differently. Don't we?

"I have endured unwanted publicity from your mistake, as Hilda loved being in the limelight. I have been in the *National Enquirer*, magazines, newspapers, and on national television. Not because I wanted to but because of your mistake. I pleaded with Jean to be discreet. I was informed, 'This is our family, and we will do whatever it takes to find our daughter and sister.' I knew this was correct. I was not their daughter.

"You can argue that my life might not have been any better in my biological family, but that question can never be answered. Your mistake has changed my life forever. You took away my father and grandmother since they passed away before I could meet them. If we can't settle my case, I can tell a jury about my life. Then you can explain to them how it was not your fault. And that I have not suffered or lost anything."

As I finished speaking, I looked around the table, and there was not a dry eye. Within half an hour, my case was settled. I was so happy and exhausted at the same time. After three years of battling the legal system, it was finally over. Everyone shook hands and left the room. John, Scott, and I remained.

Scott started laughing, saying, "Millions of dollars were on the table, and I was out there kicking the pop machine for a quarter."

The drive home was quiet. I silently prayed, "Thank you, God, for carrying me through some of the darkest days of my life. Amen."

A few weeks later, Scott received a shadow box frame with a quarter and a business card from Banner Health's attorney. Scott and I had a good laugh. At work, he hung it up in his office.

I wrote John and his staff a thank you note. I appreciated all they had done for me. They went above and beyond in my case. They were kind, compassionate, and patient with me. And we had all become friends while spending so much time together in the preceding three years. Then, I received a letter from John.

"Thank you for trusting and believing in us. You have exhibited the most incredible and admirable traits of the human spirit. Your spirit of survival has been gallant, and your courage is unbelievable. Your hope in the face of adversity is nothing short of heroic.

So, while we appreciate your thanks to us and say, "You're welcome," thank you for touching our lives with yours and showing us how one exhibits true courage, strength, and hope. Thank you for providing us with a great role model and hero. Your impact on our lives is beyond words. We shall remain forever grateful. We are most thankful and proud to call you our friend." John Robinson

DEBBIE

In the fall of 2006, Aunt Mary called me and said, "Debbie is sick and dying. Craig is living with her in Arizona and caring for her. But he is refusing to let anyone visit her."

I was incredulous. Raising my voice, I said, "What? Are you kidding me? How can he stop her family from visiting her? I'm going to call Polly. She needs to be with Debbie. Do you know what is wrong with her?"

Aunt Mary replied, "All I know is Craig said she had cancer. I'm happy you are going to call Polly. I just wanted to let you know. Oh, Craig said he was doing it because Debbie didn't want to see anyone."

I hung up the phone and was furious. How dare Craig keep Debbie's family from visiting her? I was bound and determined that if Polly and Jean wanted to be with Debbie, I would make it happen.

I called Polly and said, "Aunt Mary just called me about Debbie. Would you like to go and see her?"

Polly was steadfast and said, "No, I can't. Craig won't let me see her."

I was livid, and in a sharp and determined voice, I said, "Oh yes, he will. I will make sure of that. Debbie needs you right now, and you must be with her."

Polly sounded defeated. "No, Craig won't let me see her. Besides, I don't have money for a ticket."

I pleaded with her, saying, "I will pay for your ticket. I assure you Craig won't stop me. Or if you would rather, Benita can go with you, and I'll pay for her ticket, too. Debbie needs her mom right now."

Polly was adamant and said, "No, I can't go."

After our call ended, I looked at my phone. What? I was blown away by why she wouldn't want to go. Regardless of the consequences, I would move heaven and earth if it were one of my daughters. My next call was to Jean, and I recounted the conversation I had just had with Polly.

When Jean spoke, she precisely repeated what Polly had said. I said, "I'll pay for your ticket."

Jean was snide, saying, "Well, you know she wasn't really what we thought she'd be. And I really don't want to go and see her."

I was reeling after that statement. Ironically, Debbie and I had both been rejected by our mothers and families.

Jean and Hilda's search for Debbie had inflected pain and agony on me. And now, Debbie meant nothing to her. My heart ached for Debbie.

Debbie passed away on September 28, 2006. Craig never communicated any information about her death or what happened to her body. I was appalled. Why had this happened? Debbie didn't deserve any of this.

The Morgan family held a memorial service for her at the nursing home. I hesitated to attend, but I needed to be there for Polly. The night before, Scott asked me if I would like him to come with me for support. I said, "No, I'll be fine. Bill told me he would meet me there."

I walked into the nursing home where the service was held. I looked for Bill but didn't see him. I was in a panic. Finally, I saw Polly at a table and sat down with her. It was uncomfortable, and I didn't belong there. I saw the Morgan sisters seated up in the front of the room.

Debbie's obituary was read, and the pastor said Debra's sister would like to speak. Hilda took the microphone, and in a phony voice, she began, "My little sister Debra was lost..." and then she went into great detail about finding her.

"I knew the moment I saw her she was one of us, and she fit right into our family. When we sisters were all together, we talked and laughed and had so much fun. Mom and we girls went to Minnesota to visit Mom's family. Debra reminded us of Aunt Fance, who had passed away. We went on vacations together and spent hours talking. Debra was so much fun and always silly. She sounded just like all of us. I will miss Debra. I loved her so much."

Vicky spoke next. She went on and on about all the fun they had with Debra and how much she loved her. It was basically the same speech as Hilda's.

Their speeches sickened me. Where were they when Debbie died? I wanted to run out of there, but I couldn't leave Polly alone. As soon as the service was finished, I leaned over to Polly and said, "Polly, I'm sorry I can't stay any longer. Will you be all right if I leave?"

All she said was, "Thanks for coming. Don't worry. I'll be fine."

I was speed walking to the exit door. When one of my cousins touched my shoulder, fear shot through me. But he was compassionate and said, "This must have been really hard for you to attend. I respect you and want you to know you are my cousin, and nothing could change how I feel about you."

I was touched by his comment. I smiled and said, "Thank you. I really appreciate that."

When I got home, I cried tears of anger and sorrow for Debbie. We never had the bond I had hoped for. To this day, no one has any information about her death. Nor do they know where she was buried or if she was cremated. What a tragic end to her life.

CHAPTER 17

SAYING GOODBYE

Humble yourselves, therefore, under the mighty hand of God so that at the proper time he may exalt you, casting all your anxieties on him because he cares for you.

—1 PETER 5:6–7 (ESV)

LOSS OF LOVED ONES

With all good things, there will be times of sorrow. Uncle Junior, my favorite uncle, was hospitalized with terminal brain cancer in 2008. He had been diagnosed a few years before. Throughout my childhood, he gave me the love my parents could not provide me. I had to see him at the hospital, no matter my fears. I had isolated myself from the extended Morgan family for six years because I thought they would reject me.

As I opened the door to his room, I could feel the tears welling in my eyes. I quickly walked to Uncle Junior's bedside and hugged him. At that moment, I knew he still loved me.

I saw one of my uncles and his children, my cousins. They hugged me and were happy to see me. My cousin Cheryl had taken me under her wing. She said, "We have always loved you. You are very precious to Dad and all of us."

I was so choked up all I could do was nod. We spent almost every day together, catching up on our lives and reminiscing about our huge family holidays and all the fun we had. It was wonderful to feel the unconditional love I had been given.

I asked, "Uncle Junior, do you remember when I was little and you taught me how to ice skate?" He nodded. "It was a dark winter night, so cold the snow crackled under our feet when we took a step. Aunts, uncles, and cousins all went to Caballo Creek Pond by the old Morgan ranch. You guys started a bonfire and cleared the snow off the pond. We drank hot chocolate and roasted hot dogs on the fire. I put my skates on, stood up, took two steps, and I was down. You picked me up and used my stocking cap to pull me behind you until I could finally skate. When I was older, you returned my stocking cap and gloves, the letters I had written you when I first learned how to write, and the envelope with rocks I gave you. I still have everything, and at Christmastime, I display my stocking and glove as decorations. Each time I look at them, I think about you. I love you so much."

After I told the story, we all had tears in our eyes. Happy memories from my childhood centered around my cousins. I baked caramel rolls, a quiche, and homemade chicken and noodle soup to take up to the hospital for everyone to enjoy.

On December 30, 2007, Uncle Junior passed away surrounded by family. I know he is in heaven, free from pain and suffering. At his funeral, I proudly sat up front surrounded by aunts, uncles, and cousins. I had tried to take my usual place for family functions in the very back row. My cousin Cheryl came over to me and said, "Shirley, you are family. We love you, and you belong up front with us."

God used this tragedy to reunite me with my family. Blood doesn't make you family, but love from the heart does.

CHANGES IN MY FAMILY

On February 5, 2009, my daughter Lindsay gave birth to a baby boy and named him Dacian, "Dace" for short. I was able to be with her for his birth. Lindsay had been living in Fort Collins, Colorado, since 2001. Austin and I went to visit Lindsay a few times each year. Austin has always known she is his biological mother. I knew all too well the devastating effect family secrets have on you, so I was always transparent with Austin.

Four months after Dace's birth, Lindsay and Dace moved back to Gillette. I was overjoyed to be Nana again and care for another grandbaby in the family.

In the first week of August 2009, the kids and I visited the nursing home for our traditional Sunday visits. James's health had continued to decline, and he wasn't doing well.

I received a call on August 8, 2009, that James had been hospitalized. I took Dace, who was seven months old, and we went to the hospital to visit James. His bed was surrounded by his daughters and Jean.

We visited for a short time, and it was extremely uncomfortable. Then a surgeon came, and it was decided James would need a chest tube. It was time for Dace and me to leave. The following morning, I received a call saying James had passed away during the night. I had mixed feelings about it. I was sad, but I still felt the pain from his lack of affection and love for me. He had been my father for forty-three years. I didn't know what I would have done without his support before and after Chris's birth. And he continued to be an essential part of my children's lives as their favorite grandfather. Scott and I, along with our kids, attended James's memorial service.

On October 5, 2020, Chris and his girlfriend, LaTasha, had a baby girl. Her name is Irelynn Jean. Chris gave her the middle name Jean after his beloved grandmother. Irelynn not only resembles her daddy but has his personality. LaTasha's children Riley and Kylee, have added two more grandchildren to our family.

PARTING WORDS

Jean turned ninety in 2014, and her daughters planned a big birthday celebration. A few weeks before the party, Hilda was diagnosed with cancer. Scott and I walked into the party and were greeted by Hilda and her husband. I have always had a special place for Hilda's husband. I said hello to him, and we hugged.

I greeted Hilda and stood there for a couple of uncomfortable minutes. I thought she might speak to me, but she didn't. We found our children's table in the back of the room and sat down with them. After lunch, some old friends went up front and spoke about memories of Jean from childhood. I spoke with a few of my childhood friends when we were walking out of the party.

A week later, Hilda suddenly died. It was a shock to the family. After Hilda's funeral, my brother Bill called me. His voice trembled as he said, "Shirl, did you know that Mom is moving to Utah to live with Vicky?"

I could hear the sorrow in Bill's voice. He had told me he used to stay at Mom's when the roads were bad. He lived thirty-five miles east of Gillette, and he was close to Mom.

I said, "No, Bill, I didn't know that. Why is she moving?"

Bill was upset and said, "Mom said since Hilda wouldn't be there to visit her, she wanted to live with Vicky."

I knew that deeply hurt Bill, and I said, "I'm sorry she won't be here for you. Thanks for letting me know."

Before Jean moved, the kids and I would visit with her often. One afternoon, I stopped at Jean's apartment. We talked about the weather, and then Jean proudly said, "Would you like to see my photo album from my birthday party?"

I replied, "Sure."

She pointed to a shelf where the photo albums were. I opened it and paged through it. After I finished, I looked at Jean and asked, "Could I ask you a question?"

She nodded, and I continued, "Why did you wait until I left to take the family pictures?"

Jean answered viciously, "Well, you have been a spoiled rotten brat since you were born. And you still are nothing but a spoiled rotten brat. I don't want anything to do with you. But I do want a relationship with your kids."

I just sat in stunned silence. Those words were the exact ones Vicky used to describe me when she called my best friend Diane after the *Rosie Magazine* was published. I was hurt, but more than that, I was livid. I had never kept my children from her, not even after the hurtful things she said to me.

She wasn't finished with me yet. As an afterthought, she said, "Oh, you know all the gifts you made me? I don't have room to take them with me. Do you want them back?"

Standing up and walking to the door, I turned to her and said, "No. You can find someone else to give them to."

I shut her door with tears flowing down my face, and I got into my car. Those would be the last words Jean spoke to me. She had said horrible things to me before, but this one was intentionally hurtful. I would not tell my children what she said to me.

As long as my children were happy, my sacrifices were worth it. Chris and T.J. would drive ten hours once or twice a year to visit their grandmother. They would come home and tell me about their visit to Grandma's. They loved her as much as she loved them.

POLLY

Polly and I spoke maybe once every two or three months. I had given up on the idea we would have the relationship I desired. In July, Polly called me and said, "Shirley, I wanted you to know I have been saving my money and will have surgery in Denver toward the end of August."

It was now 2016. I assumed she was having surgery on her lip. I replied, "I will pray for you. I know how many problems you have had with uncontrollable nosebleeds."

The rest of our conversation was superficial. I had prayed and prayed God would bless me with a mother-and-daughter relationship, but it never happened. God must have had other plans for me.

Aunt Mary and I spoke at least once a month. We always invited Polly, but she declined each time. I'd spend a weekend at Aunt Mary's home. A week later, on September 2,

2016, Austin, a friend, and me were on our traditional Labor Day visit to Denver. I was lying outside by the pool early in the afternoon, soaking up the sun. My phone rang, and it was Aunt Mary. She sounded choked up. "Polly had been life-flighted to the hospital in Billings."

I was in a quandary. Should I return to Gillette for a six-hour drive and then to Billings for three hours? After I hung up the phone, memories overtook me. Would she even want to see me? She had so many opportunities to forge a bond with me, but she chose not to. Why would she want to see me now? I was bitter. Polly had spurned every invitation to spend time with me the last few years.

I prayed, "God, please help me. Please show me the correct path. Amen." I thought about how Austin would feel if I told him we were going home. I made my decision. We were going to stay in Colorado.

The next day, Aunt Mary called, saying, "The bleeding was out of control. The doctor wanted to cauterize the bleeding. Benita and Juan are on their way."

A few hours later, Aunt Mary called. She cried and said, "Polly does not want anything else done to save her. She is ready to die. I don't want to let her go."

Polly passed away within hours. I went to Worland for her funeral. At Aunt Mary's house, I read her obituary. It was sad. Polly's life had been reduced to four short paragraphs. It said nothing about her life, who she was, where she was born, or her birth parents. When I read the survivors, my name and Craig's weren't listed.

At the funeral, I sat in the pew with Aunt Mary, Kim, and my cousins. The feeling of being an intruder came over me. I didn't belong there.

MORE DEATH

In the summer of 2017, I was in Billings with my Aunt Mary. We were visiting my great-aunt when Aunt Mary received a call. My half brother Jon had committed suicide when his mom's death left a void he couldn't fill. Polly had always been there to take care of him, and he couldn't live without her.

After a lengthy discussion, we decided not to attend his funeral service. Jon's death closed the ties to my immediate biological family. I never got to know Polly as a mom. I had tried hard to be her daughter, but we never had a connection. She kept me an arm's length away, and I never got to know the real Polly. I was sad that the hospital's error, that one mistake, had taken Polly from me.

JEAN

My brother Bill called in mid-December 2018. "Shirl, Mom isn't expected to live much longer. Would you please come and ride with me to Utah?"

I could hear the pain and torment in his voice. It was hard to tell him no. I was nine hours away from Gillette and ten hours from Utah at Austin's hockey tournament. It felt like déjà vu of the situation I was in when Polly died. Scott would never want me to go, and he knew what would happen—a confrontation with Vicky I couldn't withstand. Filled with sorrow, I said, "Bill, I'm sorry. We are in Blaine, Minnesota, or I would go with you."

My heart broke for Bill. I should have been with him. After his call, I was overcome with memories. I lay on the hotel bed and cried for everything I had lost. Jean had been the mother who raised me. We were close when my children were young. But after our conversation in 1994, everything changed when she asked me, "Did Dad tell you he wasn't your dad?"

It got to the point where we had no connection at all. I called my children, and through tears, I told them, "Grandma is dying."

Jean passed away on December 17, 2018. Chris and T.J. were pallbearers. Scott and I went with Lindsay as we walked through the funeral home lobby. My eyes looked forward as we weaved through the crowd. We sat as far away from the Morgan family as possible. When the service ended, I found Bill. He looked shattered. I felt tears in my eyes, tears of sorrow for my little brother.

I hugged him and said, "Bill, I love you, and I'm sorry for your pain."

Bill couldn't speak. He was suffering. I felt helpless as he turned away. I took Scott's arm, and we left. Jean's death severed the tenuous thread that held me to the parents who had raised me. With James, Polly, and Jean dying, I no longer had a chance to build a loving relationship with a parent. But that also meant no more heartbreak or rejection.

CHAPTER 18

A DIFFERENT MINDSET

The Lord is at hand; do not be anxious about anything, but in
everything by prayer and supplication with thanksgiving let
your request be made known to God. And the peace of God,
which surpasses all understanding, will guard your hearts
and your minds in Christ Jesus.

—PHILIPPIANS 4:5–7 (ESV)

When I began writing my book, I thought I had already
moved on from my past. Boy, was I ever wrong. I was
forced to go back and relive traumas I had experienced,
ripping off bandages from old wounds that never healed.
I had no idea writing about my life story would bring
about so much emotion and reveal I still had a long road
to recovery. I needed professional help, so I contacted a
Christian cognitive behavioral therapist in my hometown.

In therapy sessions, I would detail about being switched
at birth and listed my life events in chronological order,
like I was presenting a PowerPoint. I was stoic as I made
statements. When asked how I felt, I shrugged and said
nothing. Suppressing my feelings was deeply ingrained,

and I truly believed I didn't feel anything. When I was told I had post-traumatic stress disorder (PTSD), I was in shock. What? How could that be possible? I wasn't in the military, a first responder, nor had I seen horrifying deaths. But now I know why my counselor said I was the poster child for PTSD.

It took more than five sessions before I began to cry because I rarely did. God had given me the ability to bury my emotions to survive. But I could no longer tamp them down. They were bursting up, and the dam broke open. God knew it was time. I was ready and could do this. That was when the floodgates flew open. What a relief I could now write those words onto paper and know it happened to me, and it wasn't my fault. This new understanding amazed me and gave me a different mindset.

In my first marriage, I had married someone like my father, who believed work came before your family. I cared for everything in our lives; I thought a wife did that. We were young and unprepared for marriage and later divorced. I only processed my first marriage and divorce thoroughly while writing this book. Ultimately, I had written ten chapters of over twenty-three thousand words about my marriage and divorce. That's how much pain it caused me. Those chapters were not included in this book, but I have realized that writing is cathartic, and publishing this book has helped me move through so many traumatic events in my life.

I've been crying more often, too. I read about the benefits of tears, which can help keep the body healthy. Emotional tears come from the same tear ducts that produce the fluid that protects our eyes. Emotional tears come from the same gland but contain different compounds from regular eye-watering.

I started reading books about suppressed trauma. I learned that suppressing your trauma takes a toll on your body, usually causing autoimmune diseases. I had a light bulb moment. In 2012, I was diagnosed with Sjogren's syndrome and rheumatoid arthritis, both autoimmune diseases.

Looking back, I realize I was also suffering from severe depression. I had no energy, was miserable, and gained forty pounds. I was ashamed and embarrassed by my appearance. I had to force myself to leave my house. Now this made sense to me. My trauma had lingering effects on my physical health.

I began physical therapy for severe pain from sacroiliac joint instability. I underwent surgeries to fuse my left and right sacroiliac joints. My physical therapist, family doctor, and therapist agreed. I should begin eye movement desensitization and reprocessing therapy, also known as EMDR. It, too, aided my healing.

I noticed all the changes happening within me. I carried myself differently; my face was more relaxed, and my eyes brighter. I went for a routine eye exam. My vision had dramatically improved. My eye doctor explained my brain was now healing from past trauma, which explained my improved vision.

The education and wisdom I have gained from researching trauma have given me hope and understanding. Situations that once consumed me no longer keep me up at night. I no longer take things personally, and I am able to process problems without getting emotionally involved.

I am aware now that my people-pleasing behavior was a trauma response, and I am able to set healthy boundaries to keep my peace. God has blessed me with the understanding that not everything that went wrong in my life was my fault.

I have learned to let go and let God take my anxieties, worries, and concerns from me. Each morning I read scriptures, do daily devotions, and pray. I had an epiphany during my prayers not long ago. For a lifetime, I had felt abandoned, unloved, and unworthy. God told me, "You are my child, and you are loved."

This writing and healing journey has been unbearable at times. It has taken me twenty-two years to find my courage to speak up and tell my story. Now, I can proudly say I am who I am despite who I used to be. I am owning my truth.

I have been reading Topher Kearby's poetry on his Facebook posts, which has touched me.

> your journey has been
> tough at times. late
> nights. early mornings.
> tears that felt as if

they would last forever.
It was heavy. almost
impossible. but you made
it through. And now you're
on the other side of it.

what's impressive about that
story, and what's beautiful
about that path is now
others have someone to
look to so they can also
see how to navigate
the storms.

your strength. your courage.
your belief that anything
is possible—is an
inspiration. (Kearby 2020)

I felt like he wrote this poem for me.

God had a plan for me to serve and bless other people. In the process, I have been blessed.

I have fulfilled my desire to have a close family and do as much as possible for each one of them. Most importantly, our children know my love is unconditional. Scott and I have taken two families and made them into one.

Our children are successful in their careers, and we are proud of them. Austin, T.J., Lindsay and Dace, Chris, LaTasha, Irelynn, Riley, and Kylee live in Gillette. Scott and I are happy we see them all the time. We aren't as fortunate with our other two daughters, Jen and her fiancé David live in Denver, Colorado, with their dogs, Piper and Porkchop. When I had surgery in Denver, Jen took care of me for two weeks. She made sure I rested and didn't do anything. Leah lives in Casper, Wyoming, with her dogs Chica and Molly. We don't get to spend as much time with the girls as we would like to, but we make the most of the time we spend together.

LaTasha, Chris holding Irelynn, Lindsay, Shirley, Scott, T.J., Austin, Dace – 2022

While writing this book, I called my cousin Kim. After a few pleasantries and catching up, I said, "Kim, I have never understood why Polly wouldn't have a relationship with me. I tried and tried, but it never worked out."

Kim responded, "I think Polly felt like in accepting you, she would have to let go of Debbie rather than embracing you and recognizing you as her birth child. Polly's way of showing love was to provide physical care for everyone. That is why, for so many years, she provided care for the elderly people."

Kim continued, "Polly was the oldest daughter. Her father left and went back to Mexico when Polly was only nine years old. Then she had to help her mom raise her siblings. When Polly was old enough, she went to work to help her mom financially. Polly didn't have any free time to make friends. As an adult, she didn't have friends, and I don't think she knew how to create those relationships. And Polly has never had any close friendships like my mom does. But you and I are extremely independent women, as are Mom, Polly, and my sister Kathy. Polly didn't feel you needed her to take care of you if that makes sense."

"Yes, it does," I said. "I have always blamed myself, thinking it was my fault that Polly never bonded with me. Thank you, I feel so much better knowing this."

The relationships I have with Aunt Mary and my cousins Kim, Nick, and Brenda are amazing. From the beginning, we each had an instant connection with each other. Through Aunt Mary, I have met more of my maternal family. Aunt Mary, Kim, and I went to a Baez Family Reunion in 2019 and met many more cousins. And what could be more wonderful than that?

I have made peace with James, Jean, Polly, and Hilda. I've learned to rely on my faith, and I know healing requires forgiveness.

On April 30, 2022, I was interviewed by *Gillette News Record*. I was fulfilling a promise I made in 2001. This was the first time I told my story to the media. It gave me strength and confidence. It was one of the most-read *News Record* stories online in 2022. Little did I know that interview would open up phenomenal opportunities for me.

On May 12, 2022, I had just submitted a rough draft of my manuscript when I was contacted by Don Anderson, an Emmy-winning TV producer living in Los Angeles. He later interviewed me for his podcast Missing Pieces—NPE Life, a podcast that curates stories about people who find out their father isn't who they thought. NPE stands for Not Parent Expected or Non-Paternity Event.

When Don interviewed me, the first round of questions was too emotional for me, and we had to stop. The next day, we finished the interview. The more I spoke, the better I felt. I found it uplifting to tell my story to an audience who could relate. My story intrigued Don so much that my interview turned into two episodes. As of March 13, 2023, my first episode became his top-streamed podcast of all time. Every time I speak to people about my story, I feel like I am freeing a piece of my past (Anderson 2022).

On February 5, 2023, I was contacted by a retired homicide detective named David. He was working with two other people who had been switched at birth. Google alerted him to my story after an article about my life was published on the same day in a popular women's magazine in the UK. When he began telling me about his client, John, I was amazed to learn that John's life story was similar to mine.

Later that month, David, John, and I had a Zoom meeting to learn more about each other. John was seventy-seven when he learned he had been switched at birth. And like me, he had a life of abuse and eventually adopted his grandson. I was shocked to hear him talk about his life. We found endless similarities in our lives.

Finding John has given me an indescribable strength, knowing that I'm not alone. What were the odds we would find each other? There is only one explanation. God brought us together. He knew how much we needed each other. Scott and I are now planning a trip to meet John in person.

My family is a chosen family, and I know now family isn't always related by blood. And to think, all of these life revelations came while writing my book. It has brought forth validation and healing. This is my truth. I have lived it and can proudly own my story. Only through my strong faith was I able to survive and now thrive.

I know my story and recovery will offer hope to the hopeless.

Writing this book has been a blessing. I know my past has a purpose, and all of the pain I endured has given me the strength and the courage to now give back to others.

ACKNOWLEDGMENTS

Without all of the prodding from my son, Austin, I wouldn't have contemplated writing a book. Then I read a post on social media from my prima (cousin), Leia Baez. She was writing a book with the help of the Manuscripts Modern Author Accelerator, and she put me in contact with the program's founder, Eric Koester. That was the beginning of my journey. From that point forward, every step fell into place. I knew writing my memoir had been God's plan.

I thought I was writing this book to help people who had suffered trauma. But God knew I had never healed myself. He used my writing as a guide for me to seek out professional help so I could heal. To say this was the most difficult endeavor in my life, would be an understatement. At times I wanted to quit, but my husband and children were there to cheer me on. They gave me the confidence I needed to continue.

Without the Manuscripts Modern Author Accelerator and my editors, Katie Sigler, Venus Bradley, and Anne Kelley, I could not have written this book. George Throne, my marketing specialist with Manuscripts, LLC, has done an amazing job helping me market my book. I want to thank each one of them for their guidance and support throughout my journey.

The one person who inspired me, gave me strength and encouragement, and spent hours working alongside me was my prima, Leia Baez. I will be forever thankful I was blessed to be her prima.

Thank you to my early supporters who preordered my book. Because of each one of you, I was able to publish *The Little Dark One*.
Duane Aaberg, Kassie Aasen, Kim Accurso, Diana Aldana, Julie Aldinger, Ryan Allen, Marie Ammann, Connie Andersen, Leitha Anderson, Will and Susan Anderson, Teri Anderson, Phoebe Anderson, Lori Andrew, Jim Andrews, Josie Apodaca, Steve Arnold, Sandra Arendsen, Pork Chop and Piper Ausenbaugh, Diann Avery, Matt Avery, Lindsay Badwound, Leia Baez, Victor Baez Jr., Barbara Barlow, Lamont Barrientos, Scott Barstad, Bonnie Baumberger, JoNell Beck, Bryce Bennett, Dalene Berger, Genia Berry, Gregg Blikre, Jill Block, Vicki Boldon, Trudi Bricker, Cindy Brooks, Mary Brown, Melanie Buchman, Tracy Burger, Clyde and Sharon Bush, Kay Carter, Louis Carter King, Rebecca Cates, John Chase, Grace Christianson, Sue Cianciolo, Tina Clark, Debbie Clements, Sonia Clements, Brenda Coates, Pam Collins, Rita Blazek, Jo Cook, Erin Cosentino, John Cosner, Judy Crist, Suzie Curtin, Rachel Cyboron, Mindy Davenport, DaNece Day, Janice Deliramich, Kathy Dell, Jennie DeLong, Angie Denny, Danielle Dillinger, Tom Dillon, Larua

Dirks-Cossitt, Pat Donathan, Dave Dorson, Margaret Drovdal, Keela Eddy, Kathleen Eliassen, Kathleen Engle, Tami Erb, Paul Erbes, Sue Evenson, Darlene Fetters, Kenda Ford, Tom Frey, Brandon Fullenwider, Gaskins, Lana, Paige Gaskins, Gwen Geis, Kevin Geis, Mickey Geis, Burt Gleason, Lance Glover, Michele Gordon, Taylor Graveman, Bridget Griffin, Donna Grindell, Kim Groves, Terry Hagen, Sandy Halbrook, Karlene Hallock, Chet Halvorson, Steve Halvorson, Darlene Hanson, Niesha Hanzlik, Stephanie Hayden, Saylor Hayes, Charleen Haynes, Krista Heiken, Kristy Henderson, Sue Hight, Tammi Hitt, Joel Hjorth, Deloris Hjorth, Nicole Holbrook, Scott Holcomb, Evelyn Holt, Cheryl Howlett, Connie Hulse, Ronda Hunter, Megan Jackson, Carol and Rick Jahn, Shanda Jensen, Krisita Jordan, Mariann Juhl Henningsen, Debbie Kasdorf, Mary Kelley, Irma Kerns, Jamie Keuck, Lezie Kinsinger, Eric Koester, Levi Krehmeyer, Martha Krein, Tammy Land, Bear Larsen, Irelynn Larsen, Merle and Hank Larsen, DeShawn Lasiter, Lonny Liljegren, Reba Lindblom, Marlene Loudan, Sandra Love, Rita Lubnau, Victor Luna, Georgia Lundquist, Teran Maliske, Karen Mapel, Dee McClure, Virginia McQuiston, Peggy Means, Diana Means, Ken Mercado, Mary Mercado, Vickie Meredith, Krista Merryman Barker, Cindy Mertz, Jackie Meyer, Deb Michaels, Jill Miller, Jody Mills, Neva Mitchard, Amanda Moeller, Kristy Mollman, Miranda Moore, Bill Morgan, Jacquelyn and Randy Morgan, Jay Morgan, Patricia Morgan, Shirley Mortensen, Irmgard Moyer, Alice Mulkey, Brenda Muñoz, Samantha Muñoz, James Murphy, Nancy Murphy, Tom Murphy, Jo Anne Necklason, Toni Nelson, Phyliss L Newson, Nicholas Nutting, Dale Oedekoven, Debbie Olson, Steve Patafio, Barbara Patenaude, Rachelle Pearson,

Diane Pennington, Hunter Peterson, Juanita Peterson, Misty Peterson, Valerie Peterson, Jo Petterson, Kay Praska, Stacy Praska, Tyler Ptacek, Linda Randen, Alisa Rangel, Jennifer Reed, Judy Riesenberg, John Robinson, Jeffrey Robinson, Jessica Rogat, Erin Rothleutner, Lenora Sanchez, Sheila Schirmer, Jeanie Schlautmann, Shawna Schrater, Betty Schuh, Arlys Semingsen, Shelia Semlek, Marianne Sheehan, Ann Shellhart, Carol Shepherd, Linda Sigman, Kelly Soule, Christina Stack, Curtis and Sharon Starkey, Debra Stearns, Tianna Stilson, Tonya Stroup, Peggy Study, Sally Suchor, Susan Szutz, David Taylor, Dee Tennant, Chuck Tesch, G Nolan Thomas, Ruth Thompson, Aleisha Trumbull, Dana Urman, Michelle Vandersloot, Zachary Viggers, Wendy Villalobos, Lisa Vnoucek, Darlene Vortherms, Cheryl Wales, Brenda Walker, Crystal Walker, Angela Wasson, Laurie Mae Wasson, Cheryl Weisenberg, Dianne While, Chalisa Williams, Jacque Williams, Linda Wilson, Donny Winger, Michele Winger Stingley, Chance Witt, Kandi Young.

APPENDIX

CHAPTER 12

McKay, Mary-Jayne. 2002. "Family Secrets: Switched at Birth." *CBS News*, December 5, 2002. https://www.cbsnews.com/news/family-secrets-switched-at-birth-05-12-2002/.

CHAPTER 13

Barnette, Martha. 2002. "The Lost Daughters." *Rosie Magazine*, November 2002.

CHAPTER 14

Klug, Rob, director. 2002. "Family Secrets." *48 Hours*. CBS. 45 min.

CHAPTER 18

Anderson, Don. 2022. "Switched at Birth." *Missing Pieces—NPE Life*. Released June 9, 2022. 38 min. 17 sec. https://npelife.buzzsprout.com/1981432/10767166-switched-at-birth-s1-ep5.

Kearby, Topher. 2020. "You're an inspiration." Facebook, June 14, 2020.

Printed in Great Britain
by Amazon

56369080R00119